PRAISE FOR T̶H̶E̶ ̶C̶R̶E̶A̶T̶I̶V̶E̶'̶S̶ MIND

"If you've ever grappled with self-doubt, fear, or imposter syndrome, and worried that you might not have what it takes to succeed as a creator, this book is for you. Through Afremow and White's curated collection of real-life stories and insights, you'll see that you're not alone, take comfort in the realization that the creative process is messy for everyone, and gain inspiration for the next step of your own creative journey."

—Noa Kageyama, PhD, faculty at the Juilliard School

"A gold mine for any creative eager to turn their dreams into a viable career! By identifying the qualities critical to commercial success—the 5 Cs—and offering intimate, accessible examples drawn from actual creative powerhouses, the authors offer a road map every artist should follow."

—Francine Mathews, *New York Times* bestselling author

"Phil and Jim's investigation into the artist's mind offers compelling insights to help creatives from all disciplines examine their approach to their craft and revitalize their creative process. It is also a valuable resource for artists seeking to further develop their resilience and fortitude."

—Gaius Charles, actor, director, and producer

"*The Creative's Mind* is a roller-coaster ride to success that you won't want to get off. It's a powerful testament to the potential of the mind. I love the 5 Cs—it's truly a masterpiece."

—Kenny Ray Powell, actor, voice artist, and retired two-sport professional athlete

"*The Creative's Mind* is a thought-provoking exploration of creativity, offering practical tips, tools, and strategies based on the 5 Cs. I find boundless inspiration in Jim and Phil's work, affirming that creativity and inspiration can indeed be decoded and tapped into by all."

—Yana Besyadynskaya, multi-award-winning opera singer

"*The Creative's Mind* won't just help would-be artists unlock the talent within—it will show them how to flourish. Combining sage and practical advice with the real-world experiences of artists, filmmakers, fashion designers, and writers, *The Creative's Mind* tears down roadblocks to creativity and fires up imagination."

—Matthew Algeo, award-winning journalist and author of *When Harry Met Pablo: Truman, Picasso, and the Cold War Politics of Modern Art*

THE
CREATIVE'S
MIND

Also by Jim Afremow and Phil White

The Leader's Mind

Also by Jim Afremow

The Champion's Mind
The Young Champion's Mind
The Champion's Comeback

Also by Phil White

Unplugged
Game Changer
The 17 Hour Fast
Waterman 2.0
Our Supreme Task
Whistle Stop

THE
CREATIVE'S
MIND

How Exceptional Artists
Think, Make, and Perform

Jim Afremow
and Phil White

BenBella Books, Inc.
Dallas, TX

BenBella Books, Inc.
8080 N. Central Expressway
Suite 1700
Dallas, TX 75206
benbellabooks.com
Send feedback to feedback@benbellabooks.com

BenBella is a federally registered trademark.

Printed in the United States of America
10 9 8 7 6 5 4 3 2 1

Library of Congress Control Number: 2024059110
ISBN 978-1-63774-688-2 (trade paperback)
ISBN 978-1-63774-689-9 (electronic)

Editing by Victoria Carmody and Elizabeth Smith
Copyediting by Amy Handy
Proofreading by Denise Pangia and Karen Wise
Text design and composition by Aaron Edmiston
Cover design by Brigid Pearson
Printed by Lake Book Manufacturing

To all who dare to create and stand brave in the arena where imagination knows no bounds—this book is for you.

Contents

THE MENTAL GAME OF CREATIVITY

Creativity takes courage.
—Henri Matisse, artist

I n the face of a blank canvas, an empty stage, or an unstarted project, fear and self-doubt can speak the loudest. But what if these moments are where creativity truly thrives? This book isn't just a spark of inspiration—it's a gold-medal guide to mastering the mental game of creativity across any art form. Learn to transform self-doubt into fuel and fear into focus, and unleash your unstoppable creative power. It's time to bring your vision to life and own the spotlight.

CREATIVITY: THE UNIVERSAL SPARK

Creativity is the power to transform ideas into reality, merging imagination with action. It's not limited to artistic expression but is also about recognizing possibilities and bringing them to life, turning visions into tangible outcomes that drive impact—and it can be a rewarding and enjoyable journey.

Think of a child playing with building blocks, constructing fantastical castles and spaceships. Or a musician experimenting with new sounds, pushing the boundaries of their genre. Consider Leonardo da Vinci, who wasn't satisfied with just capturing the human form on canvas—he envisioned flying machines, sketched intricate anatomical models, and pondered the mechanics of underwater travel.

The best part? This creative impulse is universal, waiting to be nurtured and refined. But simply having this spark isn't enough; it also requires cultivation and a wholehearted embrace. Those who do so become true innovators, leaving a lasting impact. Unfortunately, many struggle to reach their full creative potential because they lack the mental tools to overcome the inevitable challenges along the creative journey.

This is where *The Creative's Mind* comes in. Our research and interviews with twelve exceptional creators across various disciplines uncovered a common thread: mental toughness. These individuals overcame obstacles, self-doubt, and fear; their stories provide a road map to unlocking your own creative potential. We've distilled their insights into the 5 Cs of mental toughness—a framework to help you triumph over challenges and unleash your greatness.

BEYOND RAW TALENT: THE 5 Cs OF MENTAL TOUGHNESS

As you embark on the twelve journeys within this book, you'll discover that the creative landscape is a dynamic battlefield of ideas, requiring resilience, focus, and mental agility. While raw talent is a good starting point, it's merely the foundation upon which true creative success is built. To thrive, you need the armor of mental toughness. The twelve creative heroes in this book exemplify what we call the 5 Cs: Courage, Confidence, Concentration, Composure, and Commitment.

Throughout this book, you'll witness how each of these creative luminaries has leveraged these traits to achieve remarkable success. Rather than defining each C here, we invite you to uncover their meanings and applications as you progress through the chapters. By embracing and mastering these 5 Cs, you'll transform from a hesitant bystander into an unstoppable creative force, equipped to conquer the challenges and obstacles that lie ahead.

UNLEASH YOUR CREATIVE POWER

This book is your ultimate training ground, equipping you to build resilience, silence your inner critic, and fully unleash your creative power. True fulfillment comes from mastering both the journey and yourself, finding joy in the process while appreciating the recognition that follows. In the creative arena, innovation and competition reign. To thrive, you need more than raw talent; you need the mental game that helps you prevail over self-doubt, distractions, and fear. This will enable you to:

- **Rise Above Obstacles:** Develop strategies to navigate creative blocks, time constraints, imposter syndrome, shifting industry trends, perfectionism, and external pressures. Keep moving forward despite these challenges, staying focused on your vision.
- **Reach Your Potential:** Sharpen your focus, cultivate self-awareness, embrace new ideas, and deepen your understanding of both your creative process and your personal growth journey.
- **Build Lasting Fulfillment:** Effectively manage stress, stay consistently motivated, and build lasting confidence, ensuring your creative journey remains satisfying and rewarding.

Thriving in this landscape requires both individual excellence and strong collaboration. Join a local art group, participate in online forums, or collaborate with fellow creators to spark new ideas, gain feedback, and remain inspired on your creative path.

CREATIVE SPARKS AND ACTIONABLE TOOLS

Each chapter delves into the 5 Cs of mental toughness, offering insights and practical exercises from diverse creators across a wide range of disciplines—writers, visual artists, musicians, and more. These creators showcase how the 5 Cs have fueled their success, providing lessons and inspiration to elevate your creative process.

To ignite your creative spark, we've included thought-provoking questions designed to stimulate artistic growth. Use them as prompts for journal entries, group discussions, or classes to deepen your understanding.

Actionable performance psychology tools like self-talk, visualization, and mindfulness will help bridge the gap between knowledge and action. Apply these techniques to refine your creative process, enhance resilience, and elevate your artistic pursuits.

YOUR CREATIVE JOURNEY BEGINS NOW

The Creative's Mind is more than a guide—it's a powerful catalyst for transformation. Drawing on the collective wisdom of experts and the inspiring stories of creative luminaries, this book empowers you to unlock your full potential and become the creator you've always aspired to be.

Imagine a future where self-doubt is replaced with unwavering confidence, distractions fade away with laser-like focus, anxiety transforms into excitement, and challenges become stepping-stones on your creative journey. This future is within your reach.

What if the only thing holding you back from realizing your creative potential is a simple shift in mindset? Let *The Creative's Mind* be your trusted guide on this transformative journey. Embrace your creative calling and start creating today!

Chapter 1

QUIET ON SET: DESTIN DANIEL CRETTON

The boy laughs as he chases his sister and friends across the lush green grass in their Hawaiian backyard. He's not concerned with angles, framing, or zooming—that will come later. At this moment, he is capturing the delightful chaos of summer break. Unbothered by the rising heat and humidity, the friends remain deeply absorbed in creating their lively home video. Their parents, aunts, and uncles will laugh heartily later when he proudly premieres his first childhood film on the family's small color TV.

The carefree days of filming with his sister and friends sowed the seeds for Destin Daniel Cretton's future career. These early adventures ignited a passion for filmmaking, culminating in his debut short film *Short Term 12* winning the Jury Prize at the Sundance Film Festival. The feature-length version, starring Brie Larson, Rami Malek, and LaKeith Stanfield, received rave reviews. Despite numerous offers, Destin remained true to his roots, selecting projects that allowed him to reunite with collaborators from San Diego State University.

This approach resulted in the adaptation of Jeannette Walls's memoir *The Glass Castle* in 2017 and *Just Mercy* two years later. In 2019, Destin directed *Shang-Chi and the Legend of the Ten Rings*, Marvel's first movie with a primarily Asian cast, which broke the Labor Day box office record and grossed over $432 million worldwide. Destin has expanded his portfolio by executive producing *American Born Chinese*, developing the Marvel Spotlight/Disney+ series *Wonder Man*, and directing *Spider-Man 4*.

THE STRENGTH OF AUTHENTICITY

As Destin advanced in his filmmaking journey, he began to recognize that authenticity was crucial to his progression. He became ever more aware that a film's success hinges on the trust and unity of the cast and crew. Destin knew that fostering a cohesive team would require him to embrace his true self instead of conforming to industry norms. "Hopefully you get to the point where you stop pretending, stop trying to be the person that you think other people want you to be, and just start being yourself," Destin said.

His leadership on set is defined by empathy and emotional intelligence. By creating an environment where everyone feels valued and heard, Destin ensures that each cast and crew member can bring their best selves to the project.

"I like to come on set with very clear ideas, but I'm also the first person to say that I am wrong all the time," Destin said. "I actually like to be proven wrong. If somebody has a better idea, I want to hear it, whether you're an assistant or a producer. And so that is the type of healthy, creative environment that I like to be in. It's worked for me so far. I've never had a negative experience working on a movie. Each one has been wonderful in its own way. It really all comes down to respecting people and knowing that everybody is contributing to what ends up on the screen, either positively or negatively. It's equally as important that the lowest person on the totem pole feels just as respected as our A-list star."

Destin soon realized what he didn't like about the industry and how he wanted to change the game. "From an outsider's perspective, the industry can be intimidating, with a lot of hype, money, big risks, and insincere people ready to walk all over you," he said. By sticking to his core values, Destin showed how he was going to do things differently as a director. This attracted collaborators who valued authenticity and shared his commitment to meaningful storytelling. "Entering the industry with *Short Term 12*—which clearly showed who I am, what I believe, and the stories I connect with—helped me meet like-minded people," he said. "They think like me, want to use this medium to explore ideas themselves, put some positive things into the world, and use movies to allow people who otherwise might be isolated or alone to feel a little less so when they're sitting in a theater watching the stories that we put out."

Destin's openness about his struggles with self-doubt offers a powerful lesson for aspiring creatives: it's not about eliminating fear but harnessing it to fuel your passion and drive. This mindset can turn perceived weaknesses into powerful strengths, leading to greater creative breakthroughs.

"Each project that I choose has something in it that is terrifying to me, because it's something I haven't really fully explored or thought too much about," he said. "Being able to dive into it over the course of a year or two allows me to process through things, grow as a person, and understand the world a little differently. I feel very privileged to be able to do that as my job."

Authenticity is the cornerstone of Destin's storytelling. By staying true to his experiences and those of the characters he portrays, he creates films that speak to universal human emotions and struggles. His dedication to authentic storytelling deeply resonates with audiences and sets a high standard for filmmakers aiming to create meaningful work.

To achieve this, it's crucial that he creates trust and cohesion during filming. "Once I'm on set, there's a lot to be done every day," Destin said. "The adrenaline doesn't stop, but I've been lucky to work with people who are not only good at their jobs but also genuinely good people. It's easy to trust them to do the work."

⚡ CREATIVE SPARKS 1 ⚡

Think of a time when you felt fully authentic in your creative work. Consider how embracing your true self can add depth and meaning to your projects by infusing your uniqueness (what makes you different?), passions (what drives you?), and vulnerabilities (what do you fear?) into your work.

FROM BACKYARD FUN TO BLOCKBUSTERS

The joy of filmmaking that began with shooting home videos with his sister never faded for Destin. As he climbed the ranks in the industry, he remained determined to keep that same sense of delight in his films, even as the stakes increased.

Preproduction is the most challenging phase for him, dominated by constant planning and worry over uncontrollable factors, which he enjoys the least. Yet as soon as filming begins and the initial nerves fade, he compares the experience to "playing in a sandbox with adults who are free to be kids." This shift transforms the process into a joyful and creative playground.

This is similar to the sense of wonder he observed in his son, who instinctively engaged in roleplaying and acting. "I never taught my three-year-old how to start playing make-believe—he just did it. It's connected to how we learn to live as a society and empathize with each other—by imagining ourselves in other people's shoes—and I see him doing that." This concept resonated strongly with him, particularly in projects like *Just Mercy*, where actors embody their characters' emotions.

When Michael B. Jordan donned the role of lawyer and human rights advocate Bryan Stevenson and stepped into a courtroom, he was deeply immersed in another person's experience. Similarly, Jamie Foxx envisioned himself in Walter McMillian's cell so vividly that it brought him to tears. Capturing these powerful, empathetic performances on camera—and allowing others to share in these deeply human experiences—is a profoundly moving aspect of filmmaking for Destin.

You've probably read stories about directors who push their cast and crew around or heard leaked audio of a star screaming at everyone on set. For Destin, being the director isn't about acting like some domineering top dog but rather a collaborative servant leader. In fact, he even turned over his Instagram account to his crew before the release of *Just Mercy*, moving those normally behind the scenes into the spotlight.

Destin told us about the importance of respect on set, recognizing that everyone's contributions impact the final product. "As soon as the actor steps out of their trailer, they are an emotional sponge," he said. They're walking through a maze of people who are contributing positively or negatively to their psychology. Any theater actor will tell you that their performance can completely change depending on what the audience is giving back to them, and on a film set, that audience is the crew."

He recalled a crucial learning experience on a friend's project. "After *Short Term 12*, I volunteered to work on a music video that a friend of mine was directing, and nobody knew who I was on the set. I came because he needed help, and it was a low-budget thing. I was basically there as a PA, and there were two people on the set in positions of power who treated me like shit. They talked to me like I was nothing. Like I was an idiot. I took it and took it."

This was a wake-up call, showing him how detrimental such behavior can be to a production's atmosphere. Recognizing that toxic attitudes quickly spread negativity throughout the entire production, he enforces a strict no-bullying, no-asshole policy with his department heads. If anyone exhibits such behavior on set, they are promptly and politely let go.

That's why teaming up with committed, motivated, and kind individuals is a priority for him. "I work repeatedly with those who are passionate, work hard, and are good people. For me, the ability to collaborate is much more important than hiring someone who's a 'genius' but is incapable of working in a group setting," Destin said. He's fortunate that his group of friends, who he keeps making films with, also happen to be good at what they do.

✔ CREATIVE SPARKS 2 ✔

Reignite the childlike wonder that first captivated you. How can you infuse that playful essence into your current projects, even as the stakes rise? Transform your work into a vibrant playground, where creativity and joy entwine, just as Destin does with his filmmaking.

LESSONS IN VULNERABILITY

Destin's journey in the film industry has been marked by collaborations with rising stars and established talents alike, shaping his understanding of how vulnerability can be harnessed to produce powerful performances. His film *Short Term 12* was hailed by *The Ringer* in 2019 as a springboard for future luminaries like Brie Larson, LaKeith Stanfield, Kaitlyn Dever, and Rami Malek. This success paved the way for subsequent projects like *The Glass Castle*, where Destin partnered with Larson alongside acclaimed actors Woody Harrelson and Naomi Watts.

In *Just Mercy*, Destin brought together Michael B. Jordan and Best Actor winner Jamie Foxx, uniting a diverse cast under his directorial vision. Through these experiences, Destin learned the importance of openness and honesty about his own anxieties and struggles, creating an environment where collaborators could also share their vulnerabilities.

"One lesson I've relearned is that everyone is human," Destin said. "Even highly skilled people often feel insecure. Working with Academy Award winners can be intimidating, but trying to act cool or act like I'm not scared doesn't work. As soon as I'm myself and talk about my anxieties—because I get full-on anxiety attacks before every movie—it's okay."

Balancing fears and maintaining composure is crucial for Destin, especially when working with his cast and crew. "I can't show them I'm freaked out nonstop, but I'm also very honest. I tell them I'm not sleeping because I'm thinking of all the things we're up against, but I also tell them what I'm coaching myself: we're going to do it. We're going to get through this, and I'm excited about that," he said.

Destin emphasized the power of being yourself in human connections, especially in professional settings: "One thing I've noticed is that people see through someone who fakes it and acts like they're strong without admitting any vulnerability. The scariest people are those who pretend everything is perfect all the time."

"I wish people taught kids more about the power of showing their vulnerability. I am attracted to people who show their nervousness. I instantly like someone who is nervous because now I'm on the other side of the table sometimes, and people are presenting to me. If I see they're nervous, I like them. That's powerful. I listen more, and I'm rooting for them," Destin said. "It's not something you have to worry about working on, but just be brave enough to say, 'This is who I am, and I'm really nervous.'"

One might assume a director of hundreds exudes self-assurance, but Destin often battles doubts and fears during preproduction. He now views this struggle not as a curse, but as a gift.

"I put a lot of pressure on myself before any project, but for *Just Mercy*, it was definitely at another level because I respected Bryan [Stevenson]'s work so deeply and wanted to tell a story that was honest about his experience and the experience of all of his clients," Destin said. "We were telling the story of a number of people who had passed away under an unjust system. The weight of doing it right was tearing me apart. It was really hard before we started shooting, in preproduction.

"The self-doubt was intense, and my previous therapist who was working with me through a lot of this would always remind me that my anxiety wasn't negative unless it made me stop, unless it paralyzed me. Thank goodness that never happened. It was always uncomfortable, but it made me work harder, look deeper, and make sure I was doing things correctly in *Just Mercy*.

"It allowed me to lean a little more into Bryan Stevenson and ensure we were getting everything right. So, in the end, I am thankful for my anxiety because it helps me do a better job. I think that I am on a journey to continue to find a better balance because I was eating myself alive.

"Once I'm in the game, it's fine, but the lead-up just makes me want to die. When I'm in it [shooting a film] for a day or two and I know this is happening with all the actors, I start to feel everybody working together. Then it becomes the most fun job on the planet. It's extremely fulfilling, but it's all the fear leading up to it that makes me want to quit. Every time I want to quit. I want to run away."

⚹ CREATIVE SPARKS 3 ⚹

Reflect on a moment when you bravely pushed past nervousness to pursue your creative vision. How did embracing vulnerability enhance your project's depth and authenticity? Harness those feelings to forge a stronger connection with your audience and create a supportive space for your creativity to flourish.

THE PITCH NOBODY SAW COMING

Many directors dream of making a Marvel movie, but the journey is often long and challenging, requiring persistence and a unique vision. Whether making an indie film or blockbuster action movie, Destin realized that he would have to take an unconventional path in an industry dominated by outgoing, fast-talking personalities. "I want to be clear that there's nothing wrong with being an extrovert," he said. "If that's who you are, own it. If you're comfortable in front of an audience, great. But if you're not, don't see that as a negative attribute."

Describing his own demeanor, Destin said, "I probably don't have the typical personality for this industry. I was an introvert growing up, shy in college, very slow-moving. Growing up on an island, the speed of life is slower. In college, some professors subtly discouraged me from Hollywood because they didn't think I had the right personality for it."

Destin reflected on his childhood: "When I was a kid, I used to love going to the theater, and I didn't care what I was watching—I always loved it." Growing up isolated on Maui, he found solace in movies, discovering that others experienced similar emotions. "Do other people feel lonely like this? Do other people feel awkward or insecure? Movies told me others were feeling those things. In places I've never been, people were having the same emotions I was. Movies made me feel less alone in the world."

He brings this empathy into his filmmaking, aiming to connect with audiences on a personal level. "That's one of the things I try to think about with every project I'm doing. Who's the one person or group of people that could watch this movie and think, 'Oh yeah, that's me, and I'm not going through this by myself'? Because if someone can make a movie about it, there are probably lots more people going through this out there."

Destin's compassion for characters often viewed as outsiders is a consistent theme in all his films. The struggling musician in *I Am Not a Hipster*, the vulnerable and volatile teens in *Short Term 12*, the disintegrating and dysfunctional family in *The Glass Castle*, and the unlikely hero in *Shang-Chi*—all are struggling to make their way in a world that sees them as different.

His journey to directing *Shang-Chi and the Legend of the Ten Rings* involved multiple pitches, each a learning experience. "I had to pitch five different times to get the job directing *Shang-Chi*. I went through a psychological war preparing [for the first one], trying to create something I thought they would want instead of being true to myself. So I canceled my initial meeting. The exec gave me another week, and I decided to pitch exactly what I wanted, knowing it might not be what Marvel Studios wanted. My pitch was personal and vulnerable. I started with a photo of me and my dad.

"I was extremely nervous like I always am. I'm not very good with looking at people and making eye contact. So I hid behind my computer, and I had everything written down so that if I stumbled, I could just start reading. And honestly, it was uncomfortable. Sometimes I'd get a shaky voice. I left thinking, 'There's no way I got that job,' but I felt good because the pitch was a positive experience for me. Being open and honest to Marvel executives, who turned out to be amazing and empathetic, was all I wanted to do."

Reflecting on why he unexpectedly got the gig, Destin said, "Their biggest fear is a director coming in acting like they know everything. Who I am aligns with the way they work. If I had tried to be what I thought a big studio wanted, I probably wouldn't have gotten the job."

Destin's personal experiences profoundly influence his films, particularly in their representation of marginalized communities. Following Ryan Coogler's casting of Chadwick Boseman in *Black Panther*, Destin continued this push with *Shang-Chi* and *American Born Chinese*. Reflecting on these projects, he shared, "It's been much more special and impactful for me than I expected. It wasn't until I was on set with an all-Asian cast and surrounded by such a diverse crew that I realized, 'Wow, I've never experienced anything like this before.'

"I was looking into the camera screen at a normal scene of a group of young Asian characters who are just sitting at a bar, talking about life. I've never seen that represented in a movie before, so it became one of the most fulfilling experiences that I've had working on a movie."

⚡ CREATIVE SPARKS 4 ⚡

How do your distinct experiences and traits shape your creative voice? For example, a personal struggle might inspire a poignant story, or your cultural heritage might inform a unique art style. Think of a time when your personal experience added depth and resonance to a project. By embracing and celebrating these qualities, you'll foster authentic connections with your audience.

GROWTH IN EVERY FRAME

In just a few years, Destin transitioned from making short films on a shoestring budget to directing major studio films like *The Glass Castle* and *Just Mercy* and securing a Marvel movie and TV deal. In a December 2021 Instagram post, he reflected, "It feels like yesterday that I was living in an apartment with seven roommates to keep rent low, surviving on Top Ramen and ninety-nine-cent bean-and-cheese burritos, saving my money from shooting wedding videos to afford to direct my short films."

Despite reaching the upper echelon of Hollywood, Destin continues to face the evolving demands of his career. Whether it was portraying his experience working at a group care facility in *Short Term 12*, honoring Bryan Stevenson's legacy in *Just Mercy*, or directing the first MCU movie with a primarily Asian cast and crew, the challenge always begins and ends with mindset.

"The psychological battle was bigger, and the movie [*Shang-Chi*] had more money, but it's the same idea as the Olympics: it's the same pool, the same distance, and you're swimming."

In any endeavor, it's easy to get so hung up on big decisions or swept along by the pace of the process that you stop appreciating the little details that make all your hard work worthwhile. Yet even on a large-scale production like *Shang-Chi and the Legend of the Ten Rings*, which Destin finished filming in the midst of the COVID-19 pandemic during several frenetic months on location in Australia, he made an effort to slow down and savor such golden moments.

He talked about the wonder he felt in seeing his vision come to life. "Typically, by the time I got there, our director of photography and gaffer had already started with the lighting, and I saw the set for the first time. I thought, 'All these people are working on this movie that at one point was literally just me typing words onto a screen in my apartment.' And now I was walking onto the set and there it was, built. And it was really terrifying and exciting at the same time."

Destin also thrives in preparing for intimate scenes. He often creates a quiet, focused environment before actors arrive on set. "There are always a couple of scenes where I don't tell the actors what we're going to do. When they step onto the set, it's just perfect silence. Even on a big Marvel movie, that's what takes me back to the first short films I did. The craft is exactly the same as it's always been."

His ability to create settings where actors can flourish is evident throughout his films. He believes the privilege of watching them work is immensely rewarding. In highly emotional movies like *Just Mercy*, he navigates the delicate balance of direction and improvisation in performance. Jamie Foxx's intense scenes, for instance, were profoundly impactful. "Every take was magical to watch," Destin said.

He has learned something unique from every actor he has worked with. The craft of acting fascinates him, especially observing how different audiences react to various performances. "We might tweak some scenes during editing to change how a character is perceived. It's amazing how slight changes can turn a character from unlikeable to beloved."

While some directors prefer not to rewatch their films, Destin finds viewing each finished movie and its credits a way to celebrate the collective effort of the cast and crew. "When you see an actress's performance, it's often a combination of the visual of one take and the audio of another. The intensity of the schedule and the pressure, combined with the necessity for everyone to put all that aside to create something, builds a very special community. It can be very unhealthy in the wrong hands, but it can also be really, really beautiful."

One way Destin handles the expectations of directing elite talent in high-stakes films is by valuing his personality traits that others once viewed as incompatible with Hollywood. "Being an introvert or shy, or awkward in front of people, can be positive attributes. It took time for me to accept that and realize I didn't need to change who I was to be successful."

In film school, guest speakers often described industry success in ways that contradicted Destin's personality. "Networking, pitching ideas with confidence—those things made my heart jump because that's not me. I tried to be that person for a bit but quickly realized it wasn't for me. Moving back to San Diego and deciding to make films as a hobby allowed me to relax. Everything that happened after—getting into film school, selling a documentary to HBO, winning Sundance—was just icing."

For Destin, success is not about the outcome, the money, or the critical and audience response. "It has to revolve around the experience of making these movies. I think that I have been very successful in every film because the experience of making it has made me a better person. Each part of the process up until this point has been extremely beneficial to my own psychology."

⚡ **CREATIVE SPARKS 5** ⚡

Reflect on a project where the journey was as fulfilling as the result, akin to a painter relishing each brushstroke as much as the final piece. How can you integrate this joy into your creative work? Focus on the process, celebrate milestones like mastering a complex phase, and view personal growth—from acquiring new skills to overcoming doubts—as the true reward.

MAKING FILMS OR "MAKING IT"

While Destin's journey might sound like a Hollywood fairy tale, his path was far from straightforward. At various points he had considered careers as a plumber, a nurse, and even a surfer before finding his true calling in filmmaking. His father advised him to find a regular job providing a steady paycheck, which proved invaluable when Destin reached a pivotal point in his career.

"Growing up, I thought I was going to be a plumber for a long time," Destin recalled. "First it was trash collector, then it was a plumber." In Los Angeles, the first question people often ask is about one's job, which becomes a significant part of their identity. However, on Maui, conversations are more about personal well-being and daily activities. For Destin, a job was merely a means to support a life outside of work, a perspective he admired.

It wasn't as if he aspired to be a plumber; he simply sought a consistent job that would allow him to enjoy his hobbies as well. "It was like, 'What would be consistent and allow me to surf and have the life that I want?'" Although he loved making movies from a young age, it never seemed like a viable career option. When he went to college, he initially planned to become a nurse but changed to a communications degree to take film and video classes after finding them intriguing. "I thought, 'Oh, that'd be fun.' So I switched and did that."

In LA, the pressure of making it in the cutthroat film industry made Destin reconsider his father's advice. "I completely reverted back to what my dad said. And I don't think it was a bad thing. It was actually really good for me at that time to say, not that he was right and I needed to be a plumber, but that this is not healthy, chasing this dream for the idea of 'making it.'" He now advises students to avoid starting their careers with the goal of "making it" in Hollywood, because that can lead to dissatisfaction since there's no definitive point of success. "There is no 'make it.'"

For Destin, redefining why he pursued filmmaking and what he loved about it was crucial. He focused on what he could control in his art form and redefined success in a way that no one could take away from him. Otherwise, he might have quit entirely, which he didn't want. He equated this realization to his love of surfing. "If I compared myself to most surfers, I could get really discouraged and be like, 'Man, why am I even trying?' But it's fun, so even if I don't go pro and get paid for it, even if I have to buy my own surfboards, I will still go surfing because I love it."

Similarly, many people in the film industry get discouraged and quit if they don't achieve fame. Destin believes that pursuing creativity solely for fame is not a good reason. Instead, he emphasizes the importance of finding a way to keep doing what you love, no matter what the outcome is.

"If you really love a craft, you figure out a way to do it, and you just keep doing it. And then if it turns into something, that's awesome. And if it doesn't, you have this amazing creative outlet that you can keep doing for the rest of your life."

⚡ CREATIVE SPARKS 6 ⚡

Define your creative legacy: What impact do you want to leave through your work? How can you align your projects with this vision, prioritizing fulfillment and joy? By clarifying your creative purpose, you'll unlock a deeper sense of direction and motivation.

THE 5 Cs IN DESTIN DANIEL CRETTON'S JOURNEY

Destin Daniel Cretton's journey from filming home videos in Hawaii to directing blockbuster films in Hollywood exemplifies mental toughness through the 5 Cs:

1. **Courage:** Destin embodies courage by maintaining his unique directorial voice despite industry pressures. His honesty about self-doubt and fears fosters a supportive set environment, strengthening team cohesion and encouraging collective creativity and productivity.
2. **Confidence:** Destin's journey, from his breakout at Sundance with *Short Term 12* to directing major blockbusters, showcases unwavering confidence in his artistic vision. He demonstrates the importance of trusting one's instincts, underscoring the concept of self-efficacy—the belief in one's ability to succeed.
3. **Concentration:** Destin's filmmaking approach requires meticulous planning and intense focus, particularly during preproduction and on set. His ability to concentrate under pressure ensures every scene captures intended emotional depth and narrative precision, crucial in both low-budget shorts and high-stakes blockbusters.
4. **Composure:** Destin excels in managing on-set stress, maintaining composure amid chaotic demands. By acknowledging and accepting his anxiety, he navigates high-pressure environments with resilience, ensuring clear-headed decisions that foster personal growth and project success.
5. **Commitment:** Destin's dedication to authenticity and meaningful storytelling defines his career. Prioritizing narrative integrity and impact on audiences, he rejects superficial success markers. This intrinsic motivation underscores a profound commitment to his craft, inspiring perseverance and adaptability in his creative endeavors.

YOUR CREATIVE TOOLKIT

Just as Destin Daniel Cretton exemplifies the 5 Cs of mental toughness in his journey as a filmmaker, you too can develop these strengths. Here are practical tips and tools based on the 5 Cs of creativity, inspired by his journey.

1. **Courage:**
   - **Find Heroic Inspirations:** Draw inspiration from courageous characters like T'Challa in *Black Panther*, Shang-Chi in *Shang-Chi and the Legend of the Ten Rings*, or Katniss Everdeen in *The Hunger Games*. Reflect on a powerful scene from one of these movies and think about how it can inspire your next project. Let their heroic spirit spark your creativity!
   - **Fuel Your Courage:** Watch movies that showcase extraordinary bravery to fuel your creative courage. Schedule a movie night this week and choose a film that inspires you to be bold in your creative endeavors. Let the heroes' fearlessness motivate you to push beyond your comfort zone and take creative risks.
   - **Face Your Fears:** Let the resilience and boldness of these heroes inspire you to face challenges head-on and take bold steps in your creative journey. Identify a challenging task you've been avoiding and take the first step toward tackling it today. Remember, courage is not the absence of fear, but the willingness to act in spite of it.
2. **Confidence:**
   - **Model Confident Masters:** Identify individuals who exemplify confidence, whether in your life, from history, or on the big screen. List three confident role models and observe their behaviors this week. Study how they carry themselves, communicate, and tackle challenges. Let their confidence inspire and motivate you!
   - **Soak up Confidence from Personal Heroes:** Reflect on those you know personally who exude unwavering

confidence—whether an older sibling, parent, relative, friend, teacher, or colleague. Reach out to one of your personal heroes and ask about their approach to confidence. Learn from their experiences, strategies, and mindset to boost your own self-assurance.

- **Boost Your Heroic Confidence:** Look to iconic heroes like Wonder Woman and Iron Man for inspiration. Wonder Woman's courage and compassion or Iron Man's innovative spirit and resilience can be your catalyst for creative empowerment. Choose one principle or trait from one of these heroes and implement it in your daily routine starting today. Let their heroic confidence fuel your artistic expression and success!

3. **Concentration:**
   - **Study the Habits of High-Achievers:** To cultivate concentration, start by identifying individuals who exemplify extraordinary focus, whether in real life, sports, or animation. Study their approaches and identify key takeaways, such as setting clear goals, prioritizing tasks, or maintaining a strong work ethic. Adapt these strategies to fit your needs and goals.
   - **Learn from Champions:** You can also learn from legendary athletes like Tom Brady, who demonstrated remarkable concentration during game-winning drives, and rising stars like Coco Gauff, who maintains intense focus during high-stakes tennis matches. Analyze their preparation and performance techniques, and develop a greater awareness of your own concentration habits. Identify areas for improvement and work on enhancing your focus.
   - **Find Focus in Fiction:** Additionally, draw inspiration from animated heroes like Mulan, who overcome challenges and stay focused. Study their strategies and cultivate a growth mindset by embracing the idea that concentration can be improved with practice, patience, and persistence. By applying these principles, you can enhance your concentration and achieve your goals.

4. **Composure:**
   - **Choose Your Composure Role Model Wisely:** Find your composure role model by identifying individuals who exemplify exceptional calmness in real life, movies, or sports. Study their techniques for remaining calm in stressful situations, such as their body language, breathing patterns, and thought processes. Notice how they maintain eye contact, posture, and facial expressions, and how they use deep breathing, pauses, or controlled exhales to manage stress.
   - **Observe Cinematic Composure Closely:** Observe cinematic characters like James Bond or Hermione Granger, who remain unflappable under pressure. Analyze their approaches to stress, such as pausing to collect their thoughts, using positive self-talk or affirmations, and maintaining a calm tone and pace in communication. By learning from these examples, you can develop your own strategies for maintaining composure in challenging situations.
   - **Draw Inspiration from Epic Comebacks:** Relive iconic sports movie scenes where characters maintain their composure to stage epic comebacks. Reflect on the team's resilience in *Miracle*, Maggie Fitzgerald's determination in *Million Dollar Baby*, or Daniel LaRusso's focus in *The Karate Kid*. Think about how maintaining composure, like these characters, could have changed the outcome of a recent challenge. Let their examples motivate you to stay calm, focused, and creative under pressure!

5. **Commitment:**
   - **Study Commitment Icons:** Identify individuals known for their unwavering commitment and examine their goal-setting strategies, time management skills, and resilience in overcoming challenges. By understanding the drivers of their dedication, you can adopt these principles in your own life and projects.

- **Embody Resolve from Cinema:** Explore characters like Rocky Balboa or Rey from *Star Wars*. Analyze their motivational speeches, willingness to take risks, and capacity to learn from failures. This can help you strengthen your commitment and cultivate a growth mindset.
- **Take Dedication Lessons from Athletes:** Gain inspiration from athletes like Lionel Messi or Simone Biles. Introduce a new routine or habit that reflects their dedication and discipline, such as establishing a structured training schedule or dedicating time for self-reflection.

IN THE NEXT CHAPTER

Where mental toughness meets boundless creativity, step into the imaginative world of Ashley Stegon, a renowned digital artist celebrated for her breathtaking mythical designs. Explore how Ashley's resilience fuels her artistic journey, offering powerful insights to inspire and elevate your own creative pursuits.

Chapter 2

CRAFTING CINEMATIC MAGIC: ASHLEY STEGON

*S*eated before two widescreen monitors, the artist meticulously brings The Mandalorian's *iconic character to life, transforming a two-dimensional sketch on one screen into a stunning three-dimensional masterpiece on the other. She spins the hero 360 degrees, examining every angle. Later, she'll adjust the size of his breastplate, shoulder pads, and iconic helmet to ensure the next 3D-printed costume fits the actor perfectly. This is how the magic of* Star Wars *comes alive in a blockbuster TV show.*

Ashley Stegon turns childhood dreams of drawing into reality, creating mystical characters for blockbuster movies and TV shows. Her artistry breathes life into two-dimensional sketches, reworking them into three-dimensional wonders featured in the *Avengers* franchise, *The Mandalorian*, and prominent exhibits in Las Vegas.

"Art is being vulnerable and opening yourself up to people and showing them what you like and what you're interested in, and how you see the world and how you want to convey your thoughts and feelings. And it's a very personal thing," Ashley explained.

PERSISTING THROUGH CRITICISM

Ashley's creative process seamlessly blends technical precision with a dedication to originality. She constantly reflects on questions like "What is art?" and "What inspires you?" In a world driven by trends, Ashley focuses on producing high-quality, unique creations rather than merely following popular styles.

"Being an artist is about self-expression," Ashley said. "Stay true to yourself, even amid social media trends. Art isn't a popularity contest, and it's easy to get lost if you follow others too much."

Ashley emphasized the importance of creating for yourself while being inspired by others. "Don't let likes dictate your work. If you're only creating for likes, it's hard to convey your true message." She looks to better artists for inspiration without negative comparison. One of her favorites is Rob Wallace, whose work inspires her to improve. "I have to remember he's been doing it longer than I've been alive. It should be inspiring that I have twenty years to get good at this."

"It's not one size fits all; it's a constant journey," she said. "It's important to be inspired but not be a copy. Because if someone can hire Rob Wallace or me to draw like him and they have a big budget, they'll go with him. You don't want that as an artist."

When feeling down or making unhealthy comparisons, Ashley reconnects with the love of drawing from her childhood. "I used to draw dragons and dinosaurs all the time. When I feel bad about my art, I draw dinosaurs. It reminds me it's about doing what I love. As long as you have fun, you can be successful. Stress and bad comparisons stunt your growth as an artist."

Handling client critiques is crucial in Ashley's work. Understanding their vision and engaging productively, she quickly learned to manage feedback and adjust her art accordingly, all while maintaining confidence in her unique talents.

"You might think, 'I'm not good enough' when a director suggests changes," Ashley said. "But criticism is about understanding their vision. Handle it positively, focusing on conveying their ideas, not on feeling like a bad artist."

Working with directors like Tim Burton or James Cameron involves understanding very different visions. "You can't take criticism too harshly because it just means you're not understanding what they want. You need to take it as a challenge and say, 'Okay, how can I make this vision come through?'"

Recognizing the nature of criticism is crucial; not all feedback is useful. While social media opinions can often be dismissed, genuine constructive criticism is meant to foster improvement. Understanding the difference helps you focus on what truly matters in your creative process.

Ashley finds working with experienced professionals like Tim Burton particularly rewarding. "When a director has a specific vision, it can be motivating to meet their expectations. Successfully achieving their vision brings praise and growth, because each project teaches valuable lessons about collaboration.

"I worked on a Tim Burton display in a Las Vegas museum, where the challenge was to turn whimsical, sometimes nonsensical drawings into 3D characters that looked good from every angle. You try to make it something that people are going to be walking around. How do you make it look good from every angle, and get it to feel unburdened from the drawing?"

Ashley enjoyed the freedom this project provided. "I created a weird pirate suit for a crazy, long-necked guy. It was whimsical and fun. It's really cool to be able to work with people who have that much experience in the industry."

Balancing authenticity and critique is an ongoing journey for Ashley, but it's one that fuels her growth as an artist.

⚡ CREATIVE SPARKS 1 ⚡

Reflect on what ignites your creative passion. First, recall a moment when you felt fully connected to your work. Next, find ways to bring that joy into your current projects, even under pressure. Finally, identify strategies to maintain authenticity in your creative process, staying true to your vision.

TAKING SMALL STEPS TOWARD SUCCESS

While maintaining authenticity is crucial, navigating a successful career in the arts also requires practical steps. In some professions, there are clear, structured paths. For example, becoming a physician involves completing an undergraduate degree, attending medical school, and doing a residency before you're a full-fledged doctor. This progression is straightforward and well-defined.

In contrast, the path for creatives is often unpredictable. Ashley emphasized the importance of recognizing pathway markers and consistently taking small, practical steps to move forward.

"Stepping-stones have been laid out by those who came before you," Ashley said. "Research the artists you admire and be active in your goals. Don't just dream; take small, achievable steps every day to get closer to your aspirations." Studying the journeys of successful artists provides invaluable insights and guidance, helping you create a tangible path to your own aims.

This is how Ashley learned the importance of being in the moment, doing things now, and being present. This kind of mindfulness is vital to creativity and getting into the zone, that state of being outside of timeliness when you're exclusively in your own headspace.

As crucial as it is to manage your own mindset, teamwork and advancing projects as a group are also essential elements in the professional creative world. Ashley stressed the importance of building relationships, noting that while someone may not need your help immediately, they might someday. Networking can often feel daunting, especially when it requires venturing beyond familiar territory. However, as Ashley's experience shows, these connections can be pivotal. Consider your interactions as investments for the future.

"Don't be afraid to talk to people—you'll be amazed," Ashley said. "Networking is the reason why I have this job now. You have to be vulnerable at those stages, and you can't be afraid to talk to them at this time. Maybe things don't work out, but you made the connection and maybe the next day—and although I say 'next day,' that's just a metaphor for maybe a week or a month from now—something happens."

When working on big, ambitious projects, it's all too easy for a creator to become overwhelmed, particularly when it's on a prestigious production such as *The Mandalorian*. Similarly, you could get psyched out by looking at where you want to be in your career in a few years' time and the destination seeming unreachable.

Ashley has found strategies for dealing with both these scenarios. "It's always about reaching small, achievable goals to get there. There are too many times when I hear, 'I want to work at a studio.' But have you done anything to actually take steps toward that goal?' [I ask.] 'Honestly, no. Right now, I'm comfortable, so I haven't really put my mind to start being active.' It's all about taking steps toward your goal. By setting smaller steps for yourself, you make it achievable."

Ashley stressed the importance of matching ambition with action. It's easy to get comfortable and delay pursuing dreams, but consistent effort is key to success. By establishing smaller, manageable goals, the larger objective becomes less daunting and more reachable, ensuring steady progress.

⚡ CREATIVE SPARKS 2 ⚡

Identify three actionable steps today to advance your creative goals—such as sketching a new concept, reaching out to a collaborator, or sharing your work online for feedback. Use these actions to build momentum and create future opportunities.

PUSHING PAST FEAR

Ashley's father had high expectations for her—and initial fear and concern about her career choice. As Ashley noted, "He was a chemical engineer with multiple degrees, and a smart mathematician. When I told him, 'I want to be an artist when I grow up,' it wasn't the easiest conversation." However, she acknowledged that the industry offers many opportunities for artists today. "You can be an artist and do this for a living because of the way this industry has evolved. There is so much you can do with the tools available."

Ashley's experience with her father's initial skepticism reflects a common challenge for many artists—convincing others that a creative career is viable. Yet the evolving industry landscape offers more opportunities than ever before.

Seizing these chances and tackling fear are critical aspects of Ashley's journey. While you can find considerable advice on how to network, land a job, ace an interview, and secure a raise, the real challenge begins when you've been given the opportunity: The offer letter is on the table, the hiring manager says they want you, and they ask when you can start. For both newcomers and seasoned professionals, it can be a very intimidating moment.

Maybe you had just put out some feelers but weren't really thinking about packing everything in and moving on to the next position. Perhaps you're pretty comfortable with your current co-workers, who are your friends. Should all that be put aside? Or could it be that your prospective employer has given you some lofty goals—and you don't know if you can really achieve them? Ashley had some thoughts on this.

"I was nervous when I started at Legacy Effects because they get nothing but big blockbuster movie projects," Ashley said. "It was easy to think, 'I was just at school, I know these tools, but do I really know what I'm doing?' I'm surrounded by people who made the original *Jurassic Park* animatronics. They inspired my childhood and are the reason why I love dinosaurs, and now I'm working with them. That's pretty scary and intimidating. But a really important thing was to remember that Legacy asked me about that opportunity because they believed I could do it.

"When I originally thought about taking this opportunity, I didn't know if I could do it. But then I decided to just try. I think everyone will be surprised by their own abilities. Every job I've approached with some intimidation has turned out to be one of my most successful projects, like working on the *Avengers* movies. That kind of fear factor actually helps."

The fear of failure can be daunting, but it can also serve as a driving force, pushing you beyond your comfort zone. In fact, Ashley's experience shows that intimidation can be a catalyst for growth and success.

"People take intimidation as being scared," Ashley said. "Everybody approaches it differently, but you should definitely take an opportunity to say, 'This is something I haven't done before, so I've got to give it my all.' Put your head down, be thoughtful about it, and have confidence that you know enough to get the job done. That's what's always helped me."

Ashley's journey started after graduating from Gnomon School of Visual Effects, where she gained experience as a character and concept artist, sculptor, and modeler. She progressed in the film and television industry, working on Marvel's *Avengers* franchise, including *Avengers: Infinity War* and *Captain Marvel*.

In addition to contributing to projects for legendary directors Tim Burton and James Cameron and working extensively on the hit Netflix show *The Mandalorian*, Ashley has challenged herself in video game design. After working at Cold Iron, Ashley became a senior 3D character artist for Squanch Games. She is also an instructor at Gnomon. The breadth of her experiences has allowed her to develop a flexible growth mindset and remain open to applying her skills in different ways on each new project.

For example, these skills were especially crucial when transforming storyboards into 3D designs and 3D-printing custom-fitted costumes for actors like Pedro Pascal for *The Mandalorian*. "I'm at the forefront of the production," Ashley said. "The way the pipeline works is usually there's a story, an idea, and concept artists design what that idea is going to look like visually. And then that gets handed off to people like me, 3D modelers or sculptors, to fully realize it, in whatever style it is that they're doing, whether it's realistic or stylized. For example, Disney characters have a particular look. My job is to realize concepts and to make sense of the design in 3D."

Each of her roles has unique challenges. On one hand, practical effects require ensuring that suits fit actors and must consider human limitations, whereas digital effects allow more freedom to create highly detailed and realistic images. "For practical effects, there are a lot of other things to take into account, such as an actor fitting into their costume," Ashley said. In contrast, video games must function in real time. Each project has its technical hurdles, and it's her job to navigate these complexities.

"The biggest thing for me is proportion. How do I make this feel like the drawing? Because you're never going to achieve the drawing exactly, and a human has to fit into a suit," Ashley said. Adjustments are necessary, such as resizing gauntlets or helmets, to ensure the suit feels right while maintaining the essence of the original drawing.

Ashley's insight into the practical challenges of her work, such as achieving accurate proportions, sheds light on the intricacies of her craft. Balancing artistic intent with physical feasibility requires a delicate touch and innovative thinking.

"Designing something like *Star Wars* can be challenging but rewarding when Jeff Chang says, 'Yes!' It's cool because he's the art director and well known for all the *Star Wars* concepts. He's been there since the beginning. Getting his approval is like gold. You worked hard, but there's always a great reward at the end."

The validation from esteemed colleagues like Jeff Chang serves as a testament to Ashley's skill and dedication. This recognition not only boosts confidence but also reinforces the value of perseverance and excellence in one's work.

✗ CREATIVE SPARKS 3 ✗

Consider an upcoming daunting task. Ask yourself: "Can I work on this for just two minutes?" Starting is often the hardest part. Commit to a tiny timeframe, build momentum, and gain the confidence to keep going.

NAVIGATING TEAM DYNAMICS

Colleagues can be your greatest allies or toughest adversaries, and so seizing opportunities requires mastering team dynamics. In any setting, it's common to feel pressure to fit in and fear of letting others down. And conflicts between personalities—often due to envy, jealousy, or anger—can escalate in groups. This adage rings true: "The work would be great if it wasn't for the people." How do you perform your best within a team when egos, politics, and agendas come into play? Ashley learned this the hard way.

"I think more often than not, when you try your best at work, the people who need to see that you're motivated and want to get the job done right will see that," she said. But sometimes for Ashley, that wasn't the case. "At one company, everybody else had been there for ages and had years of experience. So when I came in, I was the new kid who nobody needed to listen to and the one with the least amount of experience," she said.

There are always going to be initial challenges when you're the newcomer to a seasoned team. Ashley showed perseverance and willingness to go above and beyond expectations, which set her apart but also created friction. "When I started showing that I could do the job that some people weren't capable of doing or other people struggled with, that was a salient moment," she said. "It's important to note that there were people who really didn't like me, and it was because I was going the extra mile, so maybe they lost something they'd been doing for ten years."

Navigating these dynamics requires resilience and the ability to shake off negativity. "You have to just brush it off," advised Ashley. "I'm not afraid of people who act in that way. Because I know it's just an ego thing and you can't let that get to you. Not everybody's going to like you at your job. I stay positive and bring my best, and if people get jealous of that, it doesn't make much sense to me. That's just a personal vendetta. So why should that affect me? I think it's important not to let negativity creep in. If you start seeing yourself climb up, the reason people aren't liking you is that you're doing something right."

Ashley's perspective on handling workplace negativity highlighted the importance of maintaining a positive outlook and not allowing others' insecurities to hinder your progress. "When someone's not reaching their goal and takes it out on you because you have the drive and motivation, that makes me keep fighting," she said. "On the flip side, I had more people who loved my motivation and drive, like my buddy Scott Patton. We got along well, and I always went to him with questions."

Building positive relationships with colleagues who support and mentor you can counterbalance negative interactions. "He would ask me a question, and then he would actually apply it to his own work," Ashley recalled. "And that's the kind of relationship you want to build. Don't be afraid to learn from somebody who is less experienced than you. They know something that you don't—everybody does. There's always something to learn. And I think surrounding yourself with those kinds of people is really important."

Ashley is committed to learning from the old hands she works with, because she's quite early in her career compared to many of them. Diversifying skills and continuously expanding one's knowledge base is essential.

"I'm very focused on learning new tools or new ways to do things," Ashley explained. "They'll be applicable at some point. Having those tools gives you the confidence to get the job done. If you only have a hammer and someone asks you to build a house, you won't know what to do. But if you have different tools, you'll have more confidence."

She has also realized that setbacks are a key part of her progression. "It's okay to fail," Ashley said. "But you're never going to know unless you go do it. People are so afraid to fail. When I get frustrated, I think, 'You'd be surprised, things may turn out great.' If you don't know how to do something, always seek help. I have people I go to if I can't figure it out.

"My best friend, Scott, is a big-time mentor and a huge inspiration. I used to go to him for everything because I knew he'd been in this industry longer than I'd been alive. Take those opportunities to reach out when you don't know something. Go ask somebody who does. Why not? Don't be afraid of not knowing and asking for help—that should never be an embarrassing feeling."

Seeking help is a strength, not a weakness. It fosters learning and builds strong professional relationships. Ashley explained, "In fact, because I constantly got up and asked people questions, they saw that I was really determined to make something of myself. They gave me even more chances to be okay with not knowing what I was doing, to ask more questions, learn more, then get more opportunities. It's a weird cycle you go through, of knowing and not knowing how to do stuff. It's all about being active in your failures."

✐ CREATIVE SPARKS 4 ✐

Think back to a time when team dynamics tested your ability to succeed. How did you handle it? Now, for an upcoming project, identify one practical way to build strong relationships and manage conflicts—like regularly checking in with teammates to address issues early. Turn challenges into growth opportunities, just as Ashley did.

FORGING AHEAD BY ADAPTING AND NETWORKING

The adage "The only constant is change" is especially true today. In any field, from entertainment to politics, change is relentless. Yet artists like Ashley find peace by accepting this mutability and adapting as the ground shifts beneath their feet.

"This industry is constantly moving," Ashley explained. "In the '90s, video game art was low resolution, like Lara Croft from *Tomb Raider* with triangles for boobs. And then you look across something coming out now and she looks like a human, she looks real."

Rather than being overwhelmed by technological advancements in her field, Ashley welcomes the potential they unleash. "Technology is constantly evolving, growing exponentially. To stay ahead, you have to actively embrace new technologies as tools in your arsenal. It can be intimidating, but it's also incredibly exciting. I wake up each day asking,

'What's new?' because the landscape is constantly shifting. Remaining open to discovering and enjoying new advancements is key."

Ashley's approach to embracing new technology is crucial for remaining relevant. Staying curious and proactive about learning new tools is essential, but her industry is also about people. For her, the biggest advantage of attending Gnomon School of Visual Effects was the lasting relationships she formed there.

"I wouldn't have this job if I didn't know the people I met at school," she said. "When it comes to school, most of my investment was in networking rather than learning new tools. You can easily find tutorials online. What's difficult is connecting with the right people. My advice for those entering this industry is to attend events, talks, or studio tours where you can meet industry professionals."

In high school, Ashley often sketched in her notebook and attended the CTN Animation Expo, a smaller event similar to Comic Con where many industry artists gathered. It was a chance to meet and show her work to artists like David Coleman, who "was a huge inspiration to me growing up because I love drawing animals." Meeting him and showing her sketchbook was incredibly motivating and inspiring.

"I was super nervous to show this guy my work and get some advice. He liked my work. We had a nice little thirty-minute chat. Most of the artists were cool and approachable. It really motivated me and felt really good to talk to somebody in person."

Years later, Ashley posted many of her sketches on Instagram. As a professional in the industry, she received a message from David Coleman, who told her, "You have some really killer work on Instagram. Keep it up. I really like what you're doing." Now he follows her and comments on her work. This transition—from receiving a professional's advice in high school to having him praise her work on social media—was made possible by Ashley staying active and engaged in the art community.

The continuity of Ashley's relationship with David Coleman, from mentor to supportive peer, illustrates the long-term value of developing and maintaining professional relationships. Ashley shared that these can only begin if you're willing to showcase your talent: "Going to those events is important for people who want to get into this industry. Don't be afraid to be vulnerable and show your artwork. Because that's what art is: being vulnerable and opening yourself up to people and showing them what you like and what you're interested in, how you see the world, and how you want to convey your thoughts and feelings.

"My advice is to share your stuff with everybody. Don't be afraid to post shitty artwork. Don't be afraid of what people are going to say, what people are gonna do, or who likes who. Just post it for yourself. Because I've seen a lot of progress through what I post on Instagram and shared with fellow artists, and I'm always surprised by the feedback that I get. And I think that makes me grow as an artist."

Ashley's commitment to showcasing her work, regardless of its perceived quality, has facilitated her growth and garnered valuable feedback. This openness to both praise and criticism is key to continuous improvement in the creative field.

⚡ CREATIVE SPARKS 5 ⚡

Reflect on a moment when networking or learning a new skill opened doors for you in your creative career. How did those connections or skills help you grow? This week, take a specific step to connect with a mentor or explore a new tool that could advance your work, just as Ashley did in her journey.

CREATING A SUSTAINABLE PRACTICE

A creator can only keep their mind going over the long haul if their body can support them. Like a CEO who does triathlons or an artist who takes nightly walks, Ashley finds that physical activity offers an outlet and a fun way to stay healthy. Her daily regimen also allows her to remain focused amid professional challenges and is a pathway to a clear and creative headspace.

"One of the things that puts my head on straight every morning is that I have a crazy workout," Ashley said. "I love CrossFit. Getting into the mentality of working out and keeping a healthy body and mind is important. When I started to dive into my favorite artists, [I found that] they're not the people that are drawing in a corner all the time, sitting at their computer sixteen hours a day. They have a balance."

This is essential for sustaining long-term innovation. Physical activity helps Ashley's mind switch gears, often sparking new concepts. "When I exercise, my brain's thinking about something else, and maybe a new idea. Going for a walk or run definitely helps me get into the right mindset."

Establishing prework rituals also plays a critical role in her artistic workflow. "I make coffee every morning, and that normal routine is good. Simplifying helps; having a specific objective when you sit down at your computer prevents frustration."

Ashley sets specific targets to maintain productivity and focus. "If you give yourself some sort of a prompt or objective—whether it's making a silhouette or an archetype or concentrating on one piece of your scope—it can keep you going," she said. "Achieving that little milestone halfway through the day makes you feel productive and good."

She finds that concentrating on a single task helps her stay immersed in her work. "If I'm working on hair and thinking it doesn't look right, I'm just focusing on that. I'm not worried about anything else. That's all I want to do today."

Beyond finding a work-life balance, Ashley is constantly exploring what can keep her ideas flowing, especially when time is of the essence. "What is sustainable when it comes to creativity?" she asked. "When you have to work toward a deadline, does art lose its spirit? How do professional artists stay productive over twenty-plus years?" She is determined to answer these questions as she continues to develop her skills and advance the causes she's passionate about.

Ashley reflected on her work and its broader impact: "I was really into National Geographic and wanted to be the next Steve Irwin. I always had animals in my life, as I practically grew up on farmland. My big long-term goal for art is to get people to understand what an amazing world we have and the creatures we share this planet with. I'd like my art to pay it forward to animal conservation."

She sees art as a powerful tool for change. "I love the movie Jaws, but they kill a shark in the process, and it shows the power that we have through visuals to change people's minds," Ashley said. "I would like to show why it's important to keep these ecosystems alive and breathing. And you can do that through art. It's a language that everybody speaks and, subconsciously, something that everybody can relate to."

Ashley's passion for teaching also shines through. "I used to teach kids martial arts and would love to teach them art as well. It was a great medium when I was growing up and was my therapy for a lot of things. I think it's so important to have a creative outlet. I'm so grateful that I found mine and that I get to do it as a job. Reaching kids at a young age and opening their eyes to these possibilities allows them to see that there is a life and a career in it."

Her commitment to education and conservation highlights the broader impact that creative work can have. By integrating her artistic skills with her passion for the natural world, Ashley aims to inspire future generations to appreciate and protect our planet. Looking outward to other people and nature also enables her to balance personal ambition with a bigger purpose.

✳ CREATIVE SPARKS 6 ✳

Incorporate a daily walk, workout, or stretch session into your routine and pay attention to how it affects your focus and creativity. Notice if these activities help you generate new ideas or solve creative challenges. Try experimenting with different types of physical activity to see which best fuels your creative energy and keeps you inspired over the long term.

THE 5 Cs IN ASHLEY STEGON'S JOURNEY

Ashley Stegon's path from sketching as a child to creating 3D models for blockbuster films exemplifies mental toughness through the 5 Cs:

1. **Courage:** Ashley stands out for defying industry norms and staying true to her artistic vision. Her openness to feedback and resilience against criticism highlight her courage in maintaining authenticity amid external pressures.

2. **Confidence:** Ashley's progression from sketching dinosaurs to contributing to high-profile projects like *The Mandalorian* underscores the role of confidence in her career. Her trust in her abilities, reinforced by handling feedback from directors like Tim Burton, has been crucial to her growth.

3. **Concentration:** Known for her detailed 3D modeling, Ashley exemplifies concentration by transforming sketches into intricate 3D characters. Her commitment to detail ensures the exceptional quality of her work, even under strict deadlines.

4. **Composure:** Working on high-stakes projects and receiving critiques from top directors, Ashley maintains her composure admirably. She uses constructive criticism as a tool for personal and professional growth, staying calm and focused amid challenges.

5. **Commitment:** Ashley's commitment to her career is evident through her continuous learning, networking, and mentorship pursuits. Her focus on long-term growth over immediate acclaim demonstrates her dedication to evolving and excelling in her field.

YOUR CREATIVE TOOLKIT

Just as Ashley Stegon exemplifies the 5 Cs of mental toughness in her journey as a digital artist, you too can develop these strengths. Here are practical tips and tools based on the 5 Cs of creativity.

1. **Courage:**
   - **Unveil Your Authentic Self:** Embrace openness and vulnerability in your creative work. Authenticity deeply resonates with audiences and fosters meaningful

connections. Through your art, share your personal stories, struggles, and triumphs. Allow your true self to be seen and understood through your creations.

- **Balance Structure with Flexibility:** Courageously balance structure with flexibility to adapt to new insights from your unconscious. Set clear, disciplined goals for your creative work but also allow space for spontaneity and unconscious insights. Listen to your inner voice and be willing to adjust your plans as needed to stay in harmony with your true creative impulses.

- **Prioritize Self-Validation:** Overcome the fear of others' opinions by focusing on internal validation. Use daily affirmations like, "My creativity is a gift I share, not something I need approval for." Reflect on moments of judgment and list reasons why others' opinions don't define you. Shift from seeking external approval to trusting your inner wisdom, reinforcing your authenticity and courage.

2. **Confidence:**
    - **Build Self-Belief:** Cultivate the belief in your ability to achieve specific creative tasks. Focus on your skills, practice regularly, and celebrate small victories to strengthen your confidence in your creative abilities. Tell yourself: "I believe in my creative abilities and trust in my skills."

    - **Foster Unconditional Self-Esteem:** Embrace yourself regardless of success or failure in creative endeavors. Understand that suffering and challenges often enhance self-esteem by highlighting your resilience. Remind yourself: "I value myself and grow stronger through each difficulty I overcome."

    - **Embrace Self-Acceptance:** Unconditionally accept your full humanity, recognizing that every aspect of your being—strengths, vulnerabilities, and imperfections alike—contributes to your unique identity and creative expression. Say to yourself: "I accept my full humanity, embracing all that I am, without condition."

3. **Concentration:**
   - **Simplify Tasks:** Divide your projects into smaller, manageable tasks. This helps maintain concentration without feeling overwhelmed by the need for perfection in the entire project. Remind yourself: "I approach my projects step-by-step, focusing on each task with care."
   - **Enjoy the Journey:** Concentrate on the steps and the creative journey rather than just the final product. This can help reduce the pressure to be perfect and allow for more enjoyment and innovation in your work. Say this to yourself: "I find joy and value in the creative process, regardless of the outcome."
   - **Reframe Stress:** Focus on the positives in external events to manage stress. Reframe moments as opportunities for recovery and balance. Feeling overwhelmed by a tight deadline? Take a short walk in nature to clear your head and return with fresh eyes. Remind yourself: "I use moments of overwhelm as opportunities for recovery and clarity."

4. **Composure:**
   - **Recognize Anxiety:** Start by acknowledging the presence of anxiety. Pay attention to physical symptoms like increased heart rate, sweating, and muscle tension, as well as the emotional experience of feeling anxious.
   - **Reframe the Experience:** Instead of viewing these symptoms as signs of failure or danger, reinterpret them as signals of excitement, energy, or readiness to take on a challenge. For instance, see a racing heart as your body preparing for action rather than a sign of panic.
   - **Turn Fear into Fun:** Begin with small, manageable challenges that provoke anxiety and progressively tackle more difficult situations. For example, if public speaking makes you anxious, start by speaking up in small meetings and gradually work your way up to larger audiences. These incremental steps will build resilience and composure, transforming fear into fun and growth.

5. **Commitment:**
   - **Daily Practice Ritual:** Like a Mandalorian honing their combat skills and forging their armor, commit to a daily practice routine to build and sustain your abilities. Consistency in your practice is your Beskar steel, making you resilient and ready for any challenge. This is the way.
   - **Ignite Creative Passion:** Surround yourself with sources of inspiration. Whether it's music that moves you, art that sparks your imagination, the beauty of nature, or stimulating conversations, immerse yourself in these elements and let them fuel your creative journey.
   - **Reflect on Positives:** Regularly recall and reflect on positive experiences and moments of joy in your creative journey. This practice reinforces your commitment and motivation to continue creating, providing a reservoir of positive energy to draw from during tough times.

IN THE NEXT CHAPTER

Where creative resilience meets innovation, enter the groundbreaking world of Grammy-winning composer Brian Transeau (known as BT), a pioneer in electronic music and sound design. Discover how BT's resilience and creative mastery push the boundaries of audio engineering, captivating audiences worldwide.

Chapter 3

THE MUSIC SOUNDS BETTER WITH YOU: BT

The young man's brow beads with sweat under the Maryland sun. This is the fifth lawn he has mowed today, and it's not even lunchtime. As he cuts the last neat stripe, he lets the mower's motor sputter to a stop. He glances at his hands, finally grasping the cause of his pain: a row of blisters from gripping the metal push bar too tightly. Despite the discomfort, giving up isn't an option. In just a few more weeks, he'll achieve the goal he's been working toward all summer: his very first synthesizer.

While some of his friends spent their time in each other's bedrooms listening to records by '80s pop pioneers like Depeche Mode, many more classmates were at summer camps or playing sports. Yet for a shy, introverted kid like Brian Transeau (who'd later record as BT), music was always an outlet and a comfort. Ever since his parents enrolled him in the Washington Conservatory of Music at age eight, music had become a creative puzzle he was determined to solve.

Countless hours at his keyboard, mastering scales and tackling complex arrangements, couldn't satisfy Brian Transeau's thirst for more. He took up mowing lawns to purchase a Juno-106 synthesizer and drum machine, determined to create the music that played in his head. This relentless pursuit of his passion set him on a unique path.

FINDING HIS SOUND

"My mom's a psychiatrist, my dad was an FBI agent, and my grandma was the only creator in the family," BT explained. "I was the creative black sheep. My dad brought home a microcassette recorder, and I spent two weeks recording sounds from my roller skates because it made the coolest sound I'd ever heard."

Music became a sanctuary for BT. "I didn't have a lot of friends, so I found it hard to relate to people socially. Music was always safe and gave back to me, whether hearing other people's recordings or tinkering with my own instruments. I loved electronics and building things like oscillators from RadioShack kits. Whatever I've put into music, it always gave back double." This reciprocal relationship became a cornerstone of BT's life, offering comfort and fulfillment beyond mere practice.

After releasing tracks and meeting fans after live shows, he discovered that he wasn't alone in his introversion. "Now, probably half of my audience is introverted," BT observed. This realization fostered a deep sense of camaraderie and mutual understanding between him and his fans, significantly strengthening their connection. "It's an amazing bunch of like-minded misfits and bright weirdos who love my music," BT said, reflecting on the unique bond they share.

One of the ways BT found a creative edge growing up was by developing a keen sense of self-awareness and understanding the importance of mindset. He furthered this self-education by reading about personality types and studying psychology, using the reference materials his mom put on the family's bookshelves. "I'm a shrink's kid, so I'd read all the diagnostic Merck Manuals by the time I was twelve," he said. "I've been in years of therapy and am a big believer in psychology."

Blessed with precocious talent and a preternatural ear, BT's dedication to creativity paid off when he was accepted to Berklee College of Music at the age of fifteen. Younger than most of his fellow students, he absorbed techniques for arranging, orchestration, and more, incorporating classical theory into his compositions to create a new twist on a more modern and experimental form: electronic music. One of the most important lessons he learned wasn't even about music, but rather a mindset strategy that would help him throughout his career.

"One of my teachers at Berklee had us create a composition, put it on a cassette, and drag all the MIDI files on a disk," BT said. "Then we had to present what we'd created to the class. I went first, and when I was done, he told me to drop everything—the cassette, the sheet music, and the disk—into the trash can and go back to my seat. At the time I thought, 'After all this work? You've got to be kidding!'

"Now I know that the entire exercise was about attachment. It reminds me to this day that sometimes you have a lightning rod moment of receptivity, and you're not meant to hold on to it. It was personal—just for you, and then you had to let it go. The goal of being a successful, high-functioning artist is having the antenna on and when it's time to receive, being prepared to do that."

↗ CREATIVE SPARKS 1 ↗

BT's dedication led to new opportunities, personal growth, and strong community ties. Think about a time when your own commitment led to an unexpected opportunity, a valuable personal insight, and a meaningful connection with others.

RECHARGING CREATIVE BATTERIES

After releasing several singles, BT debuted his first full album, *Ima*, in 1995. This groundbreaking work was crafted on an orange-screened monochrome PC with just 32K of RAM—less than one-thousandth of what his current computer has. *Ima*, credited by many with inventing the trance genre, arrived just as a new wave of electronic music was cresting in the UK. The album cracked the Top 50 charts, marking BT as one of the hottest young producers around.

By the time he released his follow-up LP, *ESCM*, in 1997, BT had become an in-demand remixer for the likes of Madonna, Seal, and Diana Ross. He was already a fixture on the festival scene in England, across Europe, and beyond.

Since then, he has traveled the world, performing live in arenas and clubs, recording the *Electronic Opus* LP with the City of Prague Philharmonic Orchestra, playing hours of improvisational piano for his 2023 album *The Secret Language of Trees* (which debuted as the number-one-selling electronic album on iTunes) in a Singapore studio, and creating a wildly ambitious installation soundtrack for Disney's Tomorrowland in Shanghai. While accumulating more frequent flier miles than he could ever redeem, BT has fine-tuned his self-awareness to create a jet-lag-proof routine.

"There are a lot of introverts in the electronic music community, and I'm one of them," BT said. Maintaining high performance on the road requires a disciplined routine. Without it, "you'll get worn out. That's why I've become very calculated in my habits when I'm traveling."

A key part of BT's regimen involves strong rituals around sleep. While his wife, Lacy, needs eight and a half hours, BT's sweet spot is six hours and forty-five minutes. Food also plays a crucial role. During his work on Disney Shanghai's Tomorrowland, he circumvented the negative effects of ingredients like corn and grains by bringing his own food. "Sugar makes me feel cloudy," BT explained. "So being able to bring our own food helped me survive that project."

Having performed in front of hundreds of thousands of people around the world, BT used to travel with a tour manager but now does so with Lacy, who ensures he can be at his best on stage. "She's always thinking in advance about what it's going to take for me to put on a good show because she knows me so well."

BT has learned to switch between introversion and extroversion on the road. He cherishes the experience of performing and connecting with people, describing it as the reward for a life of solitude. "To get face to face with fans and hear their stories about how they identify with this music and what it meant to them is mind-blowing," he said. These live performances provide a sense of community and shared joy that balances his solitary creative process.

After such emotionally charged interactions, BT often feels overstimulated and exhausted, partly due to his ADHD. He needs to cycle down and recharge, a balance that has allowed him to keep his energy flowing over the years. "That's how I've been able to do so many performances for such a long time."

This longevity has enabled him to make powerful connections with fans all over the world. One particularly moving interaction left a lasting impact on BT. "About four years ago, we got a box in the mail and my mom, my wife, my daughter, and I sat at our kitchen table while I opened it," BT said. "I looked at the letter that was inside and said, 'I think I should read this to you out loud.' It was from an Army veteran who had done several tours in Afghanistan. He was severely wounded in combat and suffered a traumatic brain injury.

"He said that during his eight months rehabbing at Walter Reed Medical Center, listening to my album *This Binary Universe* was one of the things that helped him make a full recovery. By the time I finished reading these four pages, we were all in tears. Then I looked deeper into the box and saw there was something at the bottom of it—his Purple Heart medal."

✍ CREATIVE SPARKS 2 ✍

All personality types can thrive creatively by balancing social interaction with time to recharge. Schedule specific times for creative work and social activities to enhance your performance. Consider setting aside "quiet hours" daily for focused work.

TURNING STAGE FRIGHT INTO TRIUMPH

As BT's career soared, he encountered the inevitable challenges of live performances. Despite his meticulous preparation, not every show went according to plan. Yet these moments of adversity became growth opportunities, teaching him valuable lessons about resilience and adaptability. In a perfect world, creators would arrive at every event well rested, alert, and ready to rock and roll. Yet any artist who regularly performs live knows that this isn't always the case. Sometimes you have to grit out your best effort despite feeling worn out or sick. BT usually spends fifteen minutes doing a calming preperformance routine, but after a red-eye flight, he shakes things up—literally.

"If I've got a show in Taipei one night and then Hong Kong the next, it can pre-bias me to be fatigued to the point that I don't feel like showing up," BT explained. "But then I remind myself that this is my job, and I'm here to perform a service. And that service is to unify people through music, to lift the energy of a room." To overcome fatigue, he drinks a double espresso, runs a couple of laps backstage, and does some burpees, elevating his pulse and getting psyched up to start.

BT often performs solo DJ or live production sets, and on other occasions he plays live with collaborators like Howard Jones and Christian Burns. Over the years, he has learned that the best shows involve a degree of risk-taking and improvisation. "In a musical performance, when you're dialed in and connected, it's teetering on the edge of falling apart," BT observed. "If you're not right on that line, it's not great. Performing with others creates a group flow where you take chances and are vulnerable."

Sporting legends such as Ted Williams in baseball and Kobe Bryant in basketball frequently emphasized their dedication to delivering their utmost every night, recognizing that it could be a fan's first or sole opportunity to witness their performance on the field or court. This commitment to excellence resonates with BT, who feels a similar obligation to his audience.

"I have to be truly on my A game and show up and give everything I can in this moment," BT said. "I just want to be additive in every situation that I find myself in."

Sometimes BT becomes so caught up in his music and the energy exchange with his audience that he loses proprioception. "One time I came off stage at T in the Park in Scotland and my tour manager came rushing up to me," BT recalled. "I'd been playing a massive Yamaha electric piano that weighed at least 250 pounds and had been kneeing it off the ground for the entire set. My knee was double its normal size."

A live performance can take an unexpected detour where the line between order and chaos isn't just blurred but obliterated. It's when faced with such setbacks that a creator's composure, mental toughness, and ability to reframe a problem are put to the ultimate test. "One time I was playing to twenty-five thousand people in Sydney," BT said. "In the middle of me playing *Flaming June*, I lost power to my drum machines, my synths, and everything else except a little piano and my monitors. I had a moment of abject panic.

"But then I thought, 'Okay, what's the opportunity here? I can freak out, I can walk off stage, I can give up. But do I have anything available to me?' I did. So I played the rest of the song on the piano. Then the sound system came back to life, and I could give the crowd the rest of the set. It was one of the most rewarding performance experiences I've ever had. Sometimes things are going to happen that remind you of how little control you really have, and you just have to bake them into the performance. I always look for the opportunity in such situations."

BT stays calm in moments when others might panic by remembering advice from mentors. "A teacher that I did all these piano recitals with once told me something: 'Never show your effort,'" BT remembered. "Another teacher said to me, 'No one knows if you break a guitar string.' Sometimes these things can take you off on wild tangents that are great."

BT displays what Ernest Hemingway called grace under pressure and Italians call *sprezzatura*—making something appear effortless. Sometimes fans would tell him after a show how much they loved a particular version of a song. BT would realize that he had freaked out a little on stage and could have pushed the performance even further. These pieces of advice help him remain composed and take challenges in his stride.

> ✗ **CREATIVE SPARKS 3** ✗
>
> Turn nerves into creative energy. Next time you feel nervous, reframe it as excitement and use that energy to boost your work!

SAVORING THE STAGE AND STUDIO

As an artist, it's tempting to rush from one show to the next without pausing to appreciate the audience connection, especially when the clock is ticking and a flight to another city or country looms. Yet just like a victorious runner taking a lap of honor after winning gold at the Olympics, BT has learned to savor a command performance and realize the true rewards of his artistic journey.

"A family friend once came to one of my shows, and afterward he said, 'You're not taking this in, are you?'" BT recalled. "And I replied, 'What do you mean?' He said, 'You played and everybody's going crazy. You just bowed and then left.'" The friend compared being on stage to being in combat—autopilot takes over, and the body performs the mechanics dissociatively. "Then he said, 'Do me a favor: just stand there for an extra two seconds when you're done next time. Take in what happened and appreciate it.'"

BT took this advice to heart. "I've learned to do that, and it's really powerful. I have moments of profound gratitude that make me remember how blessed I am to do this. People in that room might've walked in unhappy or facing life stressors that I'll never know about, and they felt elevated for the hour that I was performing."

Being grateful during a live show's adrenaline rush is one thing, but maintaining a positive view amid an artist's lifestyle is challenging. That's why BT and his wife, Lacy, share three things they're thankful for each day.

"We're always bombarded with negative messages," BT said. "Our brains are wired to take in more negative information. But if you find a few good things you've overlooked, you can reset your baseline. I think about my mother-in-law, an amputee with MS, and her incredible gratitude. I have two legs, I can walk. How can I be stressed about an email?"

BT emphasizes that thankfulness is scientifically proven to improve life quality and is a key part of his daily routine. Practicing gratitude and mindfulness forces the brain to focus on positive information, aiding future planning. "There is a faith piece in there for me too, unquestionably—those are two things that go hand in hand," he said. This practice helps him lead from a place of service instead of negativity. "That's why I make gratitude a part of my meditation and then repeat it with my family. It's an incredibly significant part of my life."

BT's ability to tour without falling apart mentally or physically stems from the calm he creates through daily habits at home. This balance didn't come immediately but from learning what works best for him over two decades.

"When I was in my early twenties, you could have lit the house on fire around me, and you wouldn't have got me up from my instrument, workstation, or whatever it was I was doing," BT said. "But at some point, I realized that while I could keep doing that, what kind of life is it? And what kind of life is it for the people around me that I love? I want to be able to have these substantive, lasting relationships where I can show up and be present. Not just with my family or my significant other but also with my friends. Now I have a wonderful two-way support system with the people in my life. I have enough bandwidth to be there for them and them for me."

The life of an award-winning musician might sound glamorous, but not every day involves playing on stage to an adoring crowd or putting the finishing touches on a bestselling album. Behind the scenes, there are countless hours of painstaking effort.

As in any profession, parts of BT's job are mundane, like meticulously sorting samples into folders for easy access during future compositions. He has cultivated a warrior's mindset to his daily routine, ensuring that the conditions for focused effort are always optimal, no matter what project he's working on or where he is in his creative process.

"I have two friends who are martial artists, and they talk about the head space they put themselves into before a fight," BT said. "It's similar for me with my music—this idea of preparation before I walk into the studio."

For BT, the "magic sauce" of consistent creativity comes from maintaining a strict morning routine. "I keep what would be considered early hours for a musician and need to be on my little bamboo cushion by 6:30 AM. Then I go through my routine of prayer, meditation, and gratitude journaling. Next, I make a cup of matcha and I'm straight into the studio."

This meticulous preparation ensures that he brings his best self to every part of his artistic process. "Forty percent of the time I have to perform perfunctory tasks. Like right now, I'm scoring a video game, so I have a director, producers, animators, and our project leader to communicate with. But I save things like this for the afternoon," he said. "My morning studio time is sacred. For that first ninety minutes after I do my morning routine, it's a creative time with no distractions. It's my most productive period of the day."

For as much time as he spends living in artistic abundance and developing fulfilling relationships with his family, friends, and fans, BT also believes in making space for some measure of moderation and even self-denial in his daily routines. He stopped drinking alcohol, embraced a largely ketogenic diet that takes into account food sensitivities he discovered, and seeks out other ways to refine his lifestyle in healthy ways.

"I'm a big believer in deprivation," BT said. "I intermittently fast and use breathing techniques. My personal goal is to work up to three breathless minutes a day."

By incorporating these practices, BT not only maintains his physical health but also sharpens his mental clarity and focus. His commitment to a disciplined lifestyle reflects his dedication to his craft, showing that true creativity often flourishes within the bounds of structure and self-control.

⚡ CREATIVE SPARKS 4 ⚡

Write down three things you're grateful for each day, like a cozy coffee shop or the soothing rhythm of rain. Reflect on how they might spark new ideas or inspiration, and record your thoughts in a journal to track your creative growth.

THE ART OF THE GROOVE

BT's creative process evolved over time, leading him to embrace both macro and micro flow states. These periods of intense focus and creativity allow him to produce his best work, balancing structured routines with spontaneous bursts of inspiration.

During the early days of his career, BT would go on composing binges, riding the wave of inspiration until he'd squeezed every last note out of himself. These intense periods of macro flow—which he described as "the phone's off the hook, dad is busy, see you in a day"—are now rare but precious. Sometimes inspiration strikes, and he must channel it into new music for as long as the current is surging through his brain. BT noted, "Macro flow is a thing that's harder to plan for because you don't know when it's going to happen. It's this thing that just magically appears."

When a flow state hits, it isn't just about getting more done or completing tasks faster. BT experiences alterations in perception and sensation that allow him to hear, feel, and experience his music in new ways. "There's a perceptual thing with my hearing that changes dramatically in a flow state," he said. "Because of the hyper-focus of flow, I can hear things that I otherwise wouldn't normally. I experience time dilation, and everything on the periphery subsides.

"Sound interactions become much more visual to me, so I like to shut my eyes when I'm listening to my music. I can see sound localization and tell when things are off or out of place. Maybe there's too much reverb, or something else is pushed back too far in the mix. Then I can go and correct it."

When BT is in a macro flow state, he can stay in the studio for up to thirty-six hours. He has learned how to maintain his concentration and high-quality output when the muse strikes, ensuring that he isn't merely working a lot but also maintaining his exacting standards. This requires understanding his physical and mental needs and not allowing distractions to creep in. "I don't need to eat, I don't need to go to the bathroom," BT said. "I don't need to do anything other than stay hydrated and take little breaks. And when I do, I'll get up, stretch out, maybe do some push-ups. I might do five to ten minutes of mindfulness. But the thing that I will not do is check email or go on the internet. These things diminish the shine of that moment."

While his bouts of macro flow only come along occasionally and are often unbidden, BT has carefully scheduled micro flow blocks so they're now a daily norm. His studio is meticulously arranged—a wall of synths on the left, dual monitors and MIDI controllers in the middle, drum machines and other instruments on the right. Like a well-organized chef's kitchen, this setup facilitates a seamless, end-to-end production process.

Whether BT is spending all day creating a beat, using his beloved Jupiter-8 to compose a new melody, or layering vocals over a burbling, analog bassline, his studio arrangement supports his creative workflow. Similar to how an Olympic athlete executes an efficient interval workout, BT has experimented to find the perfect work-to-rest ratio and uses a timer to enforce it.

BT follows the 52-17 deep work routine, which he learned from other high performers. "That means fifty-two minutes of creating and a seventeen-minute break," BT explained. When his timer goes off, he jots down ideas for his next productivity block and then steps away. He also ensures there's time for family and meaningful conversations. This balance helps him maintain a life outside of creativity, something he neglected in his younger years, paying a relational price.

While in the studio, BT often enters a "crazy space where everything I try is working and I'm in my own little world." He admits he still feels fear every time he steps away from this creative high, but taking a break gives him a fresh perspective on his music.

"There have been times when I've had an idea that I thought was brilliant, I forgot it, it went away, and that's okay," BT said. "I don't beat myself up about that." He believes in staying prepared to be a lightning rod for creativity. Before returning to work, he takes a walk, practices mindfulness, and breathes deeply to regain focus. "By the time I return to the studio, I'm back with a vengeance. It might take me thirty to forty-five minutes to return fully to where I was before, but I have a more balanced perspective and can perfect the elements of a composition."

In addition to giving him and Lacy time to catch up during and after each workday, taking daily walks together also enables BT's brain to tap into the potency of making unconscious associations between seemingly disparate ideas. He then utilizes mnemonic devices as ideas bubble to the surface, so he can put them together like well-fitting pieces in a musical puzzle when he returns to his home studio. "What I'll often do during this time is interrelate things in a way that allows me to recall them later when I'm in my studio again," he said. "By the time I get back, often that idea has compounded with others, but I still remember the core tenet of where it came from, so I have it with me."

BT finds immense inspiration from the natural world surrounding his home, which changes dramatically with the seasons. He and Lacy make it a priority to spend time outdoors, immersing themselves in this dynamic environment. "We're so blessed to live in such a pretty place, and it changes all year long," BT said. From barren trees giving way to the sounds of frogs in the woods to the arrival of pileated woodpeckers and the birth of baby fox kits, the ever-changing landscape fuels his creativity. "The natural world is just endlessly inspiring in what we hear and see."

⚡ CREATIVE SPARKS 5 ⚡

Boost your creativity by implementing a work-rest balance like the 52-17 rule (fifty-two minutes of work, seventeen minutes of rest). Use your breaks for nature walks or mindfulness practices to refresh your perspective and enhance your creative flow.

FINDING THE FIRST NOTE

Starting from scratch can be daunting, but BT views it as an exhilarating challenge. Each new project is an opportunity to explore uncharted territory and push the boundaries of his creativity. While some find writer's or musician's block paralyzing, BT embraces the chance to capture ideas from his imagination and turn them into music.

"One of the things I find so profoundly life-affirming about music is when you go to create it, you're starting from a blank page," BT said. He describes the initial feeling as a "terrifying kind of existential dread" but believes that preparedness, study, and discipline enable the magical experience where "somehow it just comes."

Persevering in a creative act and heeding James Clear's advice in *Atomic Habits* never to allow a zero day are learned skills. If BT practiced only on days when the music came effortlessly, he wouldn't have released fifteen studio albums. Instead, he ensures he always gets something done, even if it needs refining later. "The more disciplined you are on a hard day and hang in there, the more it shows up," BT said. He emphasizes the importance of vulnerability and "showing up and sucking as much as it takes" to reach a state of peak creativity.

Music producer Rick Rubin has emphasized the importance of providing a safe space for collaborators to share their most outlandish ideas. BT follows this approach, encouraging the free flow of ideas with his collaborators without fear of judgment. "One of the first baseline rules I establish is that there are no bad ideas. If you've got an idea, share it. Just get it out. And if it's not great, that's how we're going to get to the good ones. You just keep going."

BT also approaches ambitious projects by breaking them down into smaller, manageable tasks. This method prevents him from feeling overwhelmed by the enormity of a massive endeavor. "A book or an album seems like such an unobtainable goal when you set out to do it, but by breaking things up into smaller tasks you realize, 'Wow, that's how this big thing happens,'" BT said. This approach not only makes large projects feel more attainable but also keeps the momentum going.

Like any professional artist, BT dedicates most of his time and energy to creating. However, he also has other responsibilities, like negotiating contracts and updating project milestones. His motivation for these tasks is rooted in his calling. "Music has been so incredibly rewarding and has given me a sense of purpose. It allows me to communicate what's happening inside of me—my intrinsic experiences, my belief system, and how I interact with the world—in a way that I can't convey with words."

He encourages others to find their purpose as well. "When I go to a music school, people want to talk about the technical aspects of making music. But I always end up asking them why they want to do this. I challenge students to understand their 'why.' As Nietzsche said, 'He who has a why to live can bear almost any how.'"

In addition to speaking at Berklee College of Music, providing free resources online, and mentoring up-and-coming musicians, BT furthers his professional education with a growth mindset. His ongoing thirst for knowledge shows up in track names referencing things like the golden ratio and the Fibonacci sequence. "I've always been a student of music and will continue to be my entire life," BT said. "I'm constantly studying and regularly taking courses. As well as mentoring others, I'm always being mentored."

Despite early success, BT continues to challenge himself in new forms. He feels most alive when he's pushing his boundaries. "I'm most comfortable when I'm uncomfortable," BT said. "So I know that I'm growing, learning, and serving if I'm in that place. It's in moments of comfort that I'm a little more worried. I like it when I'm right at the edge of what I'm capable of."

With his early success as a trance pioneer and remixer of the biggest names in pop, it would've been easy for BT to become pigeonholed. Instead, he continues to explore new creative avenues, whether composing abstract albums like *Morceau Subrosa*, creating a modular synth-centric score for the Bollywood film *Ittefaq*, or providing the music for a Pixar animated short.

In his artist bio, BT writes about a desire to be additive, not just to the music industry but to society at large. Yes, he has worked with some of the biggest talents in the business, scored an Oscar-winning film (*Monster*), and been nominated for a Grammy (for the 2010 album *These Hopeful Machines*). But at heart, he's still that thirteen-year-old kid mowing lawns to pay for his next synthesizer, pouring all his passion, talent, and energy back into the craft that has become his life's work.

"Things are cyclical in painful and beautiful ways," BT said. He views the creative process as a loop of birth, life, death, and rebirth. His goal is to create something with a positive message that uplifts and connects people. "That's a gift I have to give and share, and so I dive into it headfirst every day and try to make that loop. Sometimes I can complete it, and sometimes I can't, but it reminds me that so much of life is like that too, and that the secret is just showing up and trying."

BT's dedication to his music and his audience drives him to get up every day and continue creating. "I'm so lucky to have people who are interested in my music, to share with people that I have this kind of commonality with. I've stood in places of struggle, defeat, and challenge in the same ways that they have. If I can inspire them, not just through music but also in how I live my life, that's what I feel called to do. So I'm going to get up every day and keep doing it until I take my last breath. That's the pact I've made with myself."

✁ CREATIVE SPARKS 6 ✁

Embrace the daily commitment to your craft, just like BT, who dedicates himself to music with passion and discipline. Reflect on how showing up every day can transform your unique talents into gifts that uplift and connect with others, leaving a lasting impact.

THE 5 Cs IN BT'S JOURNEY

BT's journey from a young boy mowing lawns to save up for his first synthesizer to a groundbreaking electronic music producer showcases the principles of mental toughness through the 5 Cs:

1. **Courage:** BT embraced his introversion to explore uncharted sonic territories fearlessly. His determination is evident from his early days, like mowing lawns to afford his first synthesizer, showcasing his readiness to defy industry norms and pursue his unique sound.
2. **Confidence:** BT's confidence in his musical abilities was honed through years of dedication and early acceptance to Berklee

College of Music at fifteen. His debut album, *Ima*, which pioneered the trance genre, reflects his steadfast belief in his artistry despite industry challenges.

3. **Concentration:** Known for his meticulous studio setup, BT's disciplined work routines, like the 52-17 work-rest balance, exemplify his ability to maintain focus. This structured approach ensures the consistent high quality of his music, even under tight deadlines.

4. **Composure:** BT's composure is tested through scenarios like technical failures during live shows. His calm response to losing power and improvising on piano highlights his ability to remain composed and adapt under stress, despite dealing with ADHD.

5. **Commitment:** From his early days earning money for equipment to maintaining a disciplined lifestyle with a ketogenic diet and daily gratitude practices, BT's commitment to music and his fans is unwavering. His long-term dedication is a testament to his drive for continual excellence in music.

YOUR CREATIVE TOOLKIT

Just as Brian Transeau (BT) exemplifies the 5 Cs of mental toughness in his journey as a Grammy-nominated composer renowned for his ground-breaking work in electronic music and sound design, you too can develop these strengths. Here are practical tips and tools based on the 5 Cs of creativity, inspired by his journey.

1. **Courage:**
    - **Fuel Your Fire:** Use the preshow jitters to transform fear into creative fuel. Let the adrenaline course through you and connect with the audience on a primal level. Fear is for the sidelines; you belong at center stage. Channel your nerves into passion and let your excitement shine.
    - **Embrace the Edge:** Teeter on the cliff of creativity. Take wild risks and embrace mistakes—they might be your best moves

yet. Unleash your full potential, and don't play it safe. Push
your boundaries and let the thrill of uncertainty drive your
innovation.

- **Play in the Unknown:** The unknown is your playground!
  Embrace the thrill—the possibilities are endless. Each
  performance is a blank canvas; paint it with something
  unexpected and magical. Let the unknown ignite your
  creative spark and drive innovation.

2. **Confidence:**

- **Champion Yourself:** Transform your mindset and boost
  self-esteem with champion self-talk. Reinforce your abilities
  and worth with affirmations that build confidence. Say to
  yourself: "I speak with kindness and compassion to myself,
  embracing my creative potential with confidence and
  enthusiasm." Start with positive self-talk to lay a strong
  foundation of confidence.

- **Trust Your Compass:** Trust is your armor. Trust your
  instincts, your skills, and your ability to handle anything.
  Believe in yourself and be unshakeable. Trust fosters
  resilience and adaptability, crucial for creative success. Tell
  yourself: "I trust my instincts, skills, and inner wisdom to
  navigate life's challenges with resilience and poise." Build
  trust in your abilities to maintain confidence through
  challenges.

- **Celebrate All Your Steps:** Build resilience by celebrating
  your failures as much as your successes. Recognize that
  both are essential for growth and learning in your creative
  journey. Remind yourself: "I celebrate every experience,
  whether success or setback, as a valuable step forward in
  my journey of growth, learning, and creative evolution."
  Recognize that both successes and failures contribute to
  your growth, reinforcing a resilient mindset.

3. **Concentration:**

- **Unlock Spontaneous Creativity:** Keep a guitar, sketchpad,
  or other creative tools within easy reach to capitalize on

spontaneous inspiration. Embrace unstructured play, allowing ideas to flow freely without forcing creativity. Leverage technology, like recording ideas on your smartphone, to preserve these moments without disrupting the creative process.

- **Immerse in Deep Focus:** Schedule uninterrupted blocks for critical projects, eliminating distractions and fully engaging in the task. This dedicated practice boosts productivity and elevates creative output, ensuring quality time for your craft.
- **Sprint to Excellence:** Divide your creative process into focused intervals with clear boundaries, minimizing distractions and enhancing productivity. Alternate structured sprints with deep work sessions to maintain high concentration and efficiency, maximizing your creative potential.

4. **Composure:**
   - **Embrace Authenticity:** Perfection is unattainable, but authenticity is within reach. Embrace your true self, celebrating your quirks and your uniqueness in your live performances. Authenticity leaves a lasting impact and resonates deeply with your audience.
   - **Transform Mistakes into Masterstrokes:** View mistakes as opportunities for improvisation and growth. Adapt, think on your feet, and turn errors into unique moments that showcase your creativity and skill.
   - **Cherish Every Performance:** Acknowledge and celebrate each time you take the stage, no matter how small the show. Every performance contributes to your growth, resilience, and artistic evolution, so cherish the experience and the connections you make with your audience.

5. **Commitment:**
   - **Visualize Your Ascent:** Create a visual tracker, such as a whiteboard or digital app, to monitor your progress on various projects. Regularly mark your achievements and milestones. This visual representation serves as a constant

reminder of your goals, helping you maintain commitment and motivation.

- **Move Your Body:** Incorporate physical activity into your routine to boost creativity and maintain commitment. Activities like brisk walks or yoga can clear your mind and enhance focus. Schedule regular breaks for mindful movement to refresh your creativity and stay dedicated to your craft.
- **Milestone Markers:** Recognize and celebrate the milestones you achieve on your creative journey. This positive reinforcement keeps you motivated and committed. At the end of each month, acknowledge your accomplishments and plan a reward for reaching key milestones.

IN THE NEXT CHAPTER

Precision meets passion in the world of Keegan Hall, where hyperrealistic drawings blur the line between art and reality. Discover how Keegan's mental toughness and emotional resilience fuel his creativity, pushing the boundaries of his craft while forging powerful connections with his audience.

Chapter 4

WHY NOT YOU: KEEGAN HALL

The boy pulls another sheet from the stack of printer paper. With a pencil, he sketches the three panels of the comic strip, outlining his hero and villain. He sets down the pencil, grabs his markers, and fills in the bold colors of each character. Some kids might have felt shortchanged with these inexpensive gifts. But for the young artist, these simple supplies have unlocked a whole new creative universe.

"I'm gonna come over and kill you." The teenage girl gasped in disbelief as her uncle's words detonated in the phone receiver. In the single-wide trailer, her young cousins cowered, sensing the tension. Joanna, born legally blind with cataracts and cerebral palsy, could feel the panic building. Keegan, who had already lost friends to addiction, now faced his uncle's drug-fueled rage. Babysitting for Keegan and Joanna while their parents were out, the older cousin took charge. She called the cops, then grabbed the kids and dashed out the door and across the trailer park to a neighbor's house.

Minutes later, sirens blared and blue lights flashed. Police surrounded a trailer one street over, calling for Keegan's uncle to come out with his hands up. "They eventually got him out and took him to jail," Keegan remembers. "That night, he hanged himself."

CONFRONTING CHALLENGES

Traumatic experiences like these leave deep imprints on a child. However, young Keegan Hall didn't know any different at the time. "I just thought, 'Everyone must deal with these kinds of things,'" he said. "In some ways I'm grateful because that adversity molded me into the person I am today." The incident with his uncle was merely one of the family issues Keegan faced growing up. His parents divorced, with his dad moving into a small travel trailer next to Keegan's grandmother in another trailer park across town. His sister's disabilities also drew unwanted attention.

"If we went out anywhere—like to the mall—I'd hear people talking, whispering, and looking at her," Keegan said. "I felt like eyes were always on me, I was always uncomfortable, and I hated everything about that. Most of my life, particularly in my younger years, it felt like I was stumbling in a dark room, trying to feel my way through it, and hoping I made it to the other side somehow without something catastrophic happening. I was too afraid to ever step into the spotlight and be great because I just wanted to disappear into the background."

To quell this sense of impending disaster, Keegan retreated into himself, seeking solace in the comic books that he bought when money allowed. At first, the original storylines of superheroes and the villains they battled were enough. But soon creativity sparked in Keegan's brain, caught fire, and illuminated the darkness.

"I'd look at the artwork and make up my own story, in a sense, based on the images," he said. "Then I'd make my own imagery based on these stories that I was creating in my head. That's how I learned to draw in the early years."

While he may not have had the luxuries that many kids take for granted, Keegan was content to continue developing his comic strips with the most basic art supplies. "I had a lot of free time, not growing up with a lot of money," he said. "I remember for my birthday one year I got a box of white paper and crayons—that was my gift."

⚊ CREATIVE SPARKS 1 ⚊

Revisit a challenging time when your creativity provided comfort or escape. What sparked your imagination? How did you adapt and transform your struggles into creative expression? Reflect on how this experience shaped your unique voice, style, and strengths. What darkness can you illuminate with your creativity today?

DISCOVERING AN ARTISTIC PATH

In happier times, Keegan's parents took him to their co-ed softball games and other rec league sports. While they played, he pulled out his paper and crayons and lost himself in creating. His parents had always complimented him on his drawings, but it wasn't until other adults noticed his art that he started to believe in his talent. "I spent a lot of time drawing, and it was really powerful for me psychologically because I would get praise from people," Keegan recalled.

When he started accompanying his parents to their Tuesday night bowling league, Keegan realized that he might be able not just to get praise for his art but also to profit from it. "I eventually figured out that I could sell some of my drawings to people there," he shared. "Maybe they were just doing it because I was a kid, but I thought, 'Man, I could make some extra money doing this, which is cool.'"

Not long afterward, Keegan taught himself how to stuff a Batman teddy bear for a school assignment. Captivated by a new challenge, he made a whole range of stuffed animals and started selling them to his parents' bowling buddies for a dollar each. This early venture into entrepreneurship made him realize that his creative efforts were appreciated by others. "It reinforced this notion that I was creating something of value for people, and that added some level of self-worth," Keegan said. These small successes helped him build much-needed confidence.

Yet although his artwork began to affirm him, Keegan remained too shy to raise his hand in class and had to overcome his natural introversion by actively joining different social circles. "Growing up, I always felt there were no kids like me," Keegan admitted. "I wasn't a strange kid, I don't think, but I was quiet. I was the captain of the basketball team, so I had jock friends. There were also my art friends. I was into skateboarding too, but those friends were into drugs, and I stayed away from all that."

Keegan became a part of these various groups, but there was nobody quite like him in any of them, sometimes making him feel like an outcast. "At least I was pretty good at these things," he said, "so it gave me the ability to make social connections that I wouldn't have been able to have otherwise."

Keegan used his drawing skills and comic strips as an escape from the chaos around him. But even as his abilities grew, he remained unsure of himself and was afraid to push his limits. Fortunately, his mom always believed in him and challenged him to reach his full potential. "I was this quiet, shy kid," Keegan said. "Whenever I said something like, 'My art's no good. I could never...' my mom would reply, 'Why can't you? Why not you? Someone's going to do that thing. Why wouldn't it be you?'"

As he progressed through high school, Keegan started to consider what he really wanted to do after graduation. His mom made it clear that whatever he chose, it would involve going to college so he could make a better life for himself. But did he trust her belief in him enough to make his childhood dreams into reality?

"Growing up, my dream was to become a Disney animator," Keegan revealed. "I thought there was something so special about taking essentially nothing, a piece of paper—and in the case of animation, lots of pieces of paper—and literally bringing it to life."

To test whether he still wanted to pursue that ambition, Keegan decided to devote himself to creating an animation for his senior project. He painstakingly drew separate frames, and once he'd put them all together at the Seattle Art Institute, a ball appeared from a blank page, grew wings, and flew around the screen. It then splashed into a pool below, after which Keegan's head popped out of the water, and he waved at the camera.

The whole scene unfolded in just thirty seconds but took countless hours to produce. "Being part of that process and creating something that looked so simple but had an emotional component was an aha moment for me," Keegan said. He realized the power of art to communicate without words.

With this animation, a cartoon, and several other strong pieces in his portfolio, Keegan applied to study art at the University of Washington and was accepted. But as affirming as this was for a high school grad who was unsure of himself, he still had to overcome the criticism of others that compounded his self-doubt.

In an introduction to drawing class, the teacher made supportive comments about everyone's drawings, until she got to Keegan's self-portrait. "She shredded mine in front of everybody," he recalled. "It was a massive blow to me as an artist and a person, and that little bit of confidence that I was gaining had just been obliterated."

Despite the scathing review, Keegan resolved to restore his self-belief and applied for the prestigious studio art program. Not only was he accepted, but he also got to go to Rome for a semester, becoming the youngest student ever selected. "I'm used to people doubting me in every aspect of my life, and I always took that as a challenge," Keegan said. "It pisses me off in a good way that motivates me. I decided to prove that art teacher wrong."

⚡ CREATIVE SPARKS 2 ⚡

Recall a moment when someone recognized your talent. How did this recognition make you feel, and how did it influence your journey? Consider the impact of this affirmation on your confidence and creative direction.

OVERCOMING DOUBT WITH DETERMINATION

As he approached college graduation, Keegan faced a dilemma: turn his drawing into a career or find another path. "I had many people telling me, 'Art isn't a real career...you're not that good...you'll be poor your whole life,' and so on," he recalled. The seeds of negativity began to sprout, leading Keegan to make the difficult decision to give up art and follow another path.

Keegan's first post-graduation job was a dream come true in a different way: working for his favorite NBA team, the Seattle Supersonics. Over five years, he took on various sales and marketing roles, eventually becoming the top salesperson. However, when Starbucks founder Howard Schultz sold the team to a consortium from Oklahoma City, Keegan chose not to follow. Instead, he returned to the University of Washington to earn his MBA. After graduation, Keegan combined his new knowledge with the skills he'd learned while working for the Sonics at a startup. He helped raise $4 million for a company that was later acquired and he gained real-world experience in all areas of the business. This included running the marketing department and advancing his sales expertise.

Things were going well, but disaster loomed. Keegan's mom, who had been battling cancer, received news that the disease had returned with newfound ferocity. "We got news that the cancer had come back and were preparing to go back through the treatment process," Keegan said. Tragically, she passed away shortly after being admitted to the hospital.

His mom's passing rocked Keegan to his core. As he tried to make sense of this loss, he thought back to his childhood art projects and how his mom always praised, encouraged, and challenged him. One evening, he decided to pick up his pencil again and sketch a picture of his favorite basketball player, Michael Jordan. He posted it on Facebook, and people responded enthusiastically, with comments like "I didn't even know you could draw. That's so cool."

One of his friends saw the post and asked if Keegan could draw his favorite football player, Kam Chancellor, offering to pay $100. Keegan was surprised and excited, thinking, "You're going to actually give me money for a drawing? This is crazy, but okay." He completed the drawing, posted it online, and Chancellor saw and shared it, helping Keegan gain traction quickly.

Before long, Keegan received another commission from Chancellor himself. At the time, Keegan had a minimal social media following and described himself as "just some dude who did a drawing." However, with Chancellor's significant audience of over half a million on Twitter (now X), each project update brought more attention to Keegan's work.

Realizing the potential, Keegan decided to provide his growing fan base with a way to purchase his prints. He learned to code and created his own website. Reflecting on this, he said, "It seemed silly at the time because there was only one thing people could buy."

As Keegan opened up a new revenue stream, he received another commission from Chancellor to draw his fiancée, now his wife. Overcoming the mental hurdles that had held him back for so long, Keegan felt liberated in his creativity in a way he'd never experienced before and saw his perspective shift.

"After my mom passed, I didn't care about all that baggage I'd carried with me for so many years," Keegan said. "It was the catalyst that allowed me to take a big step forward and really go after the things that I always wanted to do but was too afraid to."

⚡ CREATIVE SPARKS 3 ⚡

Have you taken a break from creating? Reignite your creative passion by starting a fun and engaging project. Focus on the joy of creation rather than perfection. Embrace the process and let your creativity flow freely.

CREATING WITH A MISSION

Back in high school, Keegan was inspired by his sister, Joanna, to volunteer at the Special Olympics, following in the footsteps of his mom, who coached several sports. While getting back into art as a hobby, he had an idea to combine creativity with philanthropy and his love of sports.

"I was still working a regular job, and I had no intentions of making any money off my art," Keegan said. "It wasn't even on my radar to use that as an income. Since I had my day job, I thought, 'If I could raise money for charity, that'd be pretty cool.' The idea was to do a drawing of a player, make two hundred prints, and sell them for $200 each. It'd be '200 for 200,' and then I'd donate 100 percent of that money—forty grand. I didn't know if I could do it because I was still shy and lacking in confidence."

Scrolling through Twitter one evening, Keegan saw a post from Richard Sherman, the cornerback who had recently won a Super Bowl with the Seattle Seahawks. The post promoted a charity softball game to raise funds for his foundation, Blanket Coverage.

"I thought, 'Screw it, I don't even care. I'm just going to reply to him and tell him about my idea,'" Keegan said. Sherman responded positively, writing, "Send me a DM." They exchanged messages, and Keegan shared his concept of two hundred prints for $200 each, with all proceeds going to Sherman's charity. Sherman replied, "That sounds awesome. We should do it." And with that, they were off.

The challenging part was yet to come. While Keegan initially imagined a simple drawing of Sherman, the All-Pro player had a more complex vision.

"The Seattle defensive players got in a huddle before each game started," Keegan said. "He wanted Kam Chancellor in there with him and Earl Thomas. But there wasn't a photo of that, so I had to figure out a way to get Earl into the drawing. He has all these tattoos, and I had to figure out what they would look like from the back and how the light would bounce off them while he had his arms around the other guys."

After much brainstorming and erasing, Keegan finally found the right angles and lighting for the drawing, which he had to complete before Sherman's softball game. Then it was time to promote it, and Keegan wondered whether it would sell.

"We announced the project on Monday, and friends and family started talking about it on social media," he said. "Then it made it into the local news in Seattle, and the media picked up on it. Soon it was on national and international news, and journalists were asking Richard about it in the Seahawks' preseason press conference. By the time Friday rolled around, it sold out right away on my website. I thought, 'Holy cow. There's something to this.' It showed me how powerful art could be to make really significant change."

Following the success of the Sherman project, Keegan received a letter from an old family friend. She told him that somewhere his mom was smiling, proud of her son and how he was using his gifts to help others. This handwritten note struck a deep chord with Keegan.

"I cried my eyes out," he said. "This was another one of those clues that my art was reaching people in a fairly profound way and a signal to keep marching forward. It's bigger than art."

The overwhelming response validated the #KEEGAN200 concept, and the media coverage provided Keegan with a new level of exposure. But it wasn't as if things suddenly became easy. He still had to do the work one pencil stroke at a time and make new connections to further his philanthropy.

"I think people just assume that player number one introduced me to player number two," Keegan said. "Nobody ever introduced me to anybody. I had to go to the next guy and tell them why they should work with me. I still have to do that."

One of the "next guys" after Sherman was his Seahawks teammate Russell Wilson. Coincidentally, Wilson's father had told him the same thing Keegan's mom had: "Why not you?" This phrase became the name of Wilson's foundation. Wilson and his wife, singer/entrepreneur Ciara, also encouraged Keegan to up his promotion game and increase the scope to three hundred prints for more charity funds.

"Russ said, 'Come into my office. We're going to stream this for two hours, sign the prints live, talk about sports, and hang out,'" Keegan said. "That was crazy because I was still just getting going with this thing. When we were doing our campaign and live streaming, Ciara was posting on Facebook, 'Keegan is such an amazing artist.' My mind was exploding as these things were happening. We raised sixty grand with that project."

Looking for new ways to push himself, Keegan mentioned in an interview that he wanted to partner with Eddie Vedder from Pearl Jam. The interviewer encouraged Eddie to reach out if he saw the video.

"I posted that little clip on social media and tagged Eddie and his wife, Jill," Keegan said. "She replied right away and wrote, 'This is awesome.' She and I had several phone calls to put this thing together. I asked if we could shoot a thirty-second promo video to kick off the campaign. They invited me, my wife, and my daughter to their house, and we hung out with their family all night."

With more than enough footage, Keegan was ready to launch a new collaboration. Though he initially planned to charge his usual price for each print, Jill suggested they try $500 due to Pearl Jam's dedicated fan base and the charitable initiative. Despite his concerns about the high price, the prints sold out instantly, raising $100,000 in just ten seconds. Clearly, creating with a mission in mind can have a significant impact.

"I've always believed that the more we give, the more we get," Keegan stated. "My journey back to art was born from the commitment of giving back and continues to this day. As a result, over $600,000 has been raised for charity." (As of the writing of this book, it has now increased to more than $800,000.)

⚡ CREATIVE SPARKS 4 ⚡

Visualize the powerful impact your art can have. How can your unique skills and perspective drive meaningful change in the world? Define the transformation you want to ignite through your work—and take decisive action to make it a reality.

GOING ALL IN

With the 200 for 200 initiative gaining momentum and media attention, Keegan faced a pivotal decision: return to his predictable day job or fully commit to his art. He chose the latter, despite the uncertainties.

"A lot of people think they don't have options, so they end up taking the first train that comes along, living a life they have no control over, feeling like victims of circumstance," Keegan said. "But it's never too late to write the book that was meant to be written. You can always start over."

Keegan's focus on intentional improvement led him to fully commit to his art. "I went all in on art. I finally took on complete accountability. I'm going to win or lose based on me, and I'm okay with that. I'm not going to let myself lose. Even if I wasn't the most talented person, nobody was going to outwork me."

Choosing to pursue art full time was daunting, but a quote from Steve Jobs from an interview with the Santa Clara Valley Historical Association inspired him: "Life can be much broader once you discover one simple fact: Everything around you that you call life was made up by people that were no smarter than you and you can change it, you can influence it, you can build your own things that other people can use. Once you learn that, you'll never be the same again."

Having decided to go all in, Keegan realized the traditional way through the art world wasn't for him. "If you want to succeed in art, there's only one way to do it and that's through galleries," he said. "I love sports and music, and no gallery is going to hang a picture of Michael Jordan. Pencil drawings are scoffed at. I knew right away I wasn't going to try that route, so I had to create my own path."

As he started building his business, Keegan was careful to avoid comparing himself to his peers. "If you're always looking at other people and trying to emulate their success, you're not going to get anywhere. Figure out how to do this and put together your own puzzle."

Acknowledging that he would have to pursue a direct-to-consumer model, he embraced innovation, sharing behind-the-scenes content to connect with his audience. "In an age of internet shallowness, I chose depth and substance," Keegan said. "Sharing my process helped me build an audience that resonated with my story.

"If you could just cultivate one thousand true fans who will support you in anything you do and buy every new thing you put out, you can survive off those numbers. People always want to think it's all or nothing. Understanding that gives you confidence in knowing that it's possible."

Even as his skills developed, early successes with collaborations didn't guarantee long-term results. "When I got a big project, I thought, 'I just made it.' But the next day it goes back down to zero. Perseverance is key to keep getting up and trying again."

"I was a pessimist growing up because I would always prepare myself for the worst in every situation," Keegan said. "That just holds you back. Once my mom passed, I stopped caring about all these negative things. I don't care if that person thinks I'm a loser, I don't care if I fail at this thing, and if people think my artwork sucks, that's fine. I'll keep creating and putting more positivity out there, trying to inspire other people to chase their ambitions and goals."

⚡ CREATIVE SPARKS 5 ⚡

Recall a time when fear of judgment held back your creativity. How can you reframe that to free your true expression? Focus on your unique strengths and take small steps to nurture them. Gradually share your work to build confidence and turn self-doubt into pride in your perspective.

MAKING MAGIC

Keegan speaks at schools to inspire students to break through limitations. "I want young kids to take off. Society prepares people for a certain path in life. You can make your life. To not seize that opportunity is the worst jail." He hopes his life story inspires them to pursue a life of passion and purpose, but he emphasizes that choosing a creative path isn't easy. It requires doubling down, sacrificing, and betting on oneself to unveil what mindfulness expert George Mumford calls "the masterpiece within."

"Magic doesn't just happen," Keegan said. "You have to take ownership and take action. I believe in this so profoundly that I put it on the box

I send my prints out in and even got it tattooed backward on my chest in Leonardo da Vinci's handwriting: Magic is something you make."

That being said, no creator goes from beginner to master overnight. "Whenever we start something new, we're bad at it. You have to embrace being terrible and know it's part of the process. Just get started and be terrible." Fear of failure often leads to risk aversion, which prevents people from maximizing their potential. Keegan overcame this by embracing bold risk-taking and ambitious projects, exemplified by his renowned pencil drawing of Michael Jordan's iconic free-throw line dunk.

"My idea was to blur all the people out and just focus on Michael," Keegan said. "But I thought, 'Why am I so afraid of doing this?' I erased most of what I'd already drawn and redid it." The result, after 250 hours, was a hyperrealistic drawing that garnered worldwide media attention. A few years later, Keegan was commissioned to create an original drawing for Jordan, presenting it in person at his Florida golf course.

In 2016, Keegan received a request from the Washington governor's office to create a unique gift for President Barack Obama. Despite tight deadlines and an upcoming flight, Keegan's wife convinced him to seize the opportunity.

"I drew eighteen hours a day on back-to-back days," Keegan said. "It was a marathon session, but I pushed through it." The artwork was delivered to the governor, who presented it to Obama the next day.

Keegan's ability to complete such ambitious projects stems from his regimented approach and distraction-free creative space. "I have a studio at my house, and it's my safe space. I take frequent breaks and listen to podcasts and audiobooks while working."

Balancing his art with family time, Keegan adjusted his schedule. "In the early days, I'd draw all night after working all day, but I was missing time with my family. Once I went all in on art, I started getting up early and drawing all day. By the time my family gets home, I've already done a full day's work and can spend time with them."

Keegan's journey from aspiring Disney animator to successful artist involved creating comic books and cartoons as a child, enduring the ups and downs of art school, and temporarily pursuing another direction. This diversion taught him valuable skills that prepared him to build his art business. Now, he lives his mission of giving back while doing what he loves and providing for his family.

"I want you to chase your dream," Keegan said. "It's a long process, but if you believe it's possible, then it's attainable. You can create your own path and build it as you go, but you must be intentional, commit, persevere, and believe. Why not you?"

Keegan's journey exemplifies that magic is not stumbled upon; it is crafted through unwavering dedication and a relentless pursuit of one's passions. His story is a testament to the power of intentionality, resilience, and the belief that anyone can create their own magic with the right mindset and effort.

✄ CREATIVE SPARKS 6 ✄

Embrace Keegan's spirit and create your own magic! Develop a personal motto, such as "Hustle. Heartbeat. Hit Repeat," to fuel your creativity and keep you inspired.

THE 5 Cs IN KEEGAN HALL'S JOURNEY

Keegan Hall's path from sketching comic strips as a child to becoming a renowned artist exemplifies mental toughness through the 5 Cs:

1. **Courage:** Despite a tumultuous family background, Keegan found refuge and expression in art, using creativity as a brave outlet for personal traumas. His courage is evident in the way he transforms difficult experiences, like his uncle's actions, into powerful visual art.
2. **Confidence:** Keegan's self-belief grew from modest beginnings, from selling drawings at a bowling alley to collaborating with icons. His artistry gained recognition, notably through his

portrait of Kam Chancellor, which solidified his confidence and presence in the art world.

3. **Concentration:** Keegan exemplifies concentration, focusing deeply while blocking out distractions to create hyperrealistic drawings. Particularly visible in detailed projects like his intricate portrayal of Michael Jordan is his capability for intense focus.

4. **Composure:** Facing personal tragedies, Keegan maintained his composure by channeling his emotions into his art. The loss of his mother, while profoundly challenging, was met with resilience, allowing him to transform grief into creative momentum and push his artistic limits.

5. **Commitment:** Keegan's commitment to his craft is relentless, shown by his decision to pursue art full time and his involvement in charitable endeavors. His #KEEGAN200 initiative, which raised funds for charity through his art, underscores his dedication to making a positive impact through his work.

YOUR CREATIVE TOOLKIT

Just as Keegan Hall exemplifies the 5 Cs of mental toughness in his journey as an artist, you too can develop these strengths. Here are practical tips and tools based on the 5 Cs of creativity, inspired by his journey.

1. **Courage:**
   - **Unlock Creative Vaults:** Engage in practices like active imagination (visualizing freely without limits), meditation (focusing inward to clear the mind), or dream journaling (writing down your dreams upon waking) to explore your unconscious mind. These practices help unlock hidden wells of creative inspiration.
   - **Illuminate Your Unconscious:** Set aside quiet time each day to reflect on your dreams and spontaneous ideas. Capture key images, emotions, or phrases before they fade—these

fleeting moments can serve as the seeds for groundbreaking ideas.

- **Harness Courageous Insight:** It takes courage to treat your dreams and spontaneous thoughts as valuable sources of inspiration. By boldly exploring these uncharted territories, you go beyond the ordinary and open yourself to extraordinary possibilities.

2. **Confidence:**

- **Visualize Your Masterpiece:** Close your eyes and vividly imagine your completed project, whatever its form—writing, music, innovation, or beyond. See it in its entirety, with all its intricate details, harmonious elements, and vibrant energy. Feel an overwhelming sense of pride and acco...plishment. Repeat this affirmation to yourself: "I envision my completed project in vivid detail, taking pride in its precision and cohesion."

- **Showcase Your Creativity:** Imagine showcasing your art to the world, receiving positive feedback, and inspiring others. Let this visualization fuel your confidence. Tell yourself: "I present my work confidently, uplifting and engaging those around me."

- **Visualize Success Daily:** A few times each day, spend twenty-five to thirty seconds visualizing your success and the steps to achieve it. See yourself confidently completing each step. Remind yourself: "Every day, I clearly imagine my success, moving toward my goals with assurance."

3. **Concentration:**

- **Keep a Champion's Focus:** Challenge yourself to dedicate a specific timeframe, like two hours, to a single creative task. Eliminate all distractions—no phone notifications, no social media, just you and your art. This "Champion's Challenge" hones your concentration and allows for deep immersion in the creative flow.

- **Engage Intentionally:** This approach isn't just about time; it's about intention. Establish a clear structure for your creative sessions to fully engage with your art. Minimize distractions and maximize productivity by setting clear goals and sticking to them.

- **Reward Your Effort:** While the real reward lies in the creative journey itself, consider setting a small post-completion treat, like listening to your favorite music or enjoying a special snack. This extrinsic motivator can add a touch of fun and fuel your focus during the challenge.

4. **Composure:**
   - **Laugh Through Mistakes:** Sometimes laughter really is the best remedy. Finding humor in mistakes lightens the mood and makes them less daunting. Say to yourself: "I embrace the absurdity of mistakes and find the lesson in the laughter."
   - **Embrace Learning Opportunities:** Mistakes are valuable learning experiences. Each one brings you closer to mastering your craft. Remind yourself: "Every mistake moves me toward creative mastery."
   - **Practice Self-Compassion:** Be kind to yourself. Everyone makes mistakes, and they are a natural part of the creative process. Treat yourself with kindness and respect, just as you would a close friend: "I trust myself to learn and grow from every experience."

5. **Commitment:**
   - **Balance Inspiration with Discipline:** Combine creative sparks with focused effort. Begin your day with an hour of brainstorming or free writing, then transition into methodical tasks. Like the complementary duo of Dionysus (wild inspiration) and Hephaestus (steady craftsmanship), great creativity flourishes with both ecstatic insight and disciplined effort.
   - **Take the Pillow Test:** Each night, ask yourself: "Did I do my best today?" Reflect on your efforts and progress toward your creative goals. This daily self-assessment fosters consistent growth, accountability, and a commitment to

excellence. Knowing you did your best gives you peace of mind, regardless of circumstances or results, as you drift off to sleep.

- **Elevate Your Craft:** After finishing a project, assess two or three strengths ("Ups"), like using a new design software feature, and areas for improvement ("Forwards"), such as brainstorming more unique concepts. Use these insights to set clear goals for your next project, ensuring ongoing skill growth.

IN THE NEXT CHAPTER

Grace meets greatness in the extraordinary story of Suzannah Bianco, where Olympic gold and Cirque du Soleil magic converge. Join Suzannah on her inspiring journey, exploring how her remarkable mental discipline and emotional resilience propelled her to the pinnacle of her sport and the world stage, unlocking powerful lessons to help you reach your own full potential.

Chapter 5

PERFORMING FOR FLOWERS: SUZANNAH BIANCO

The eight women, clad in the iconic red, white, and blue swimsuits of Team USA, lie on their backs in the pool, legs together and arms outstretched. From an overhead view, they form a perfect wheel, their feet meeting in the center and hands touching around the perimeter. Eight creators move and breathe as one for the pinnacle event of their lives: the Olympic final. In this defining moment, the fusion of physical performance, teamwork, and artistic expression is seamless.

For anyone who has watched synchronized swimming (aka artistic swimming), it's impossible not to be amazed at how the athletes move gracefully in tandem. Suzannah Bianco won gold medals for Team USA at the 1994 World Aquatics Championships and the 1996 Atlanta Olympics in this discipline that's a unique blend of art and sport. Later, in what was almost a chance recruitment, she joined Cirque du Soleil as an on-stage performer, which became a new creative journey that lasted for twenty-three years.

Suzannah's story reveals how a young girl who followed her big sister to the pool eventually became an Olympian. She attributes her success to gratitude, openness, and an intrinsic motivation, traits that sustained her long career with Cirque du Soleil. As Suzannah's story shows, these are X factors that nurture the creative mind day in and day out.

THE PRIVILEGE OF PERFORMING

Suzannah's journey to becoming an Olympic gold medalist and Cirque du Soleil performer is a testament to persistence and creativity. Her parents instilled a commitment to persevere, ensuring neither she nor her sister gave up easily. This unwavering support and determination became the bedrock of Suzannah's success, driving her to push through obstacles and continually strive for excellence.

"I started when I was eight years old," Suzannah said. Growing up in the Bay Area, she was fortunate to be able to join the Santa Clara Aquamaids synchronized swimming team with her sister, because one drop-off was more convenient for their mom than Suzannah trying something else in a different location. She was quickly hooked, finding a unique allure in the sport that combined athleticism with artistry.

"There was a lot of creativity and freedom to move," she recalled. The sport encourages athletes to go all out, and progression, though challenging, is always achievable. Suzannah quickly excelled due to her physical advantages—like straight legs and large, symmetrical feet—and supportive team.

A persistent mindset played a crucial role in her ability to stay focused and dedicated through the years. "Like many young athletes, I found that one key to success is not giving up. Many people have stories like 'I was good, but then I got distracted.' My parents never let me quit on a whim," Suzannah explained.

This early lesson not only gave Suzannah a solid foundation for her decorated synchronized swimming career but also set the stage for when she later joined Cirque du Soleil. Her longevity there was fueled by appreciating the opportunity to connect with a new audience every performance. "I have that perspective of 'I only get to do it twice a night,' and that's a privilege," she said. "Being fully in love with what you're doing and having a purpose, such as providing for my family, is essential." Her dedication was not solely for personal satisfaction but also driven by a deeper motivation, providing for her loved ones.

She underscored the importance of having a clear and compelling reason to stay committed, which sustains long-term dedication and success. "I see people who don't know why they're there. Some find it, some don't. Part of longevity is finding your reason. I love the water and being able to get in it every night. It's hard, especially with small children, but I've come to realize this is a privilege." Revealing a profound understanding of the importance of finding fulfillment in consistent practice, she asked, "How do you find joy in doing the same thing every day?"

Suzannah compared her rigorous practice sessions to daily routines: "Everyone does the same thing every day, no matter what. Working at Cirque du Soleil gave me the freedom to train, explore other areas, and pursue other passions."

Suzannah reflected on her career and aspirations this way: "People ask, 'What do you want to do when you grow up?' I'm doing that. There's work in everything. If you find the fun, you're good." Her perspective shows the importance of enjoying one's work, making the journey as rewarding as the destination.

✎ CREATIVE SPARKS 1 ✎

Reflect on three recent moments of creative joy. Write down what sparked your excitement, like discovering a new color palette or solving a tricky plot twist. Use these reflections to reignite your passion and drive.

CRAFTING AN OLYMPIAN MINDSET

Persistence in her early years laid the foundation for Suzannah's Olympic success, but her mental fortitude truly set her apart. Reaching an elite level relies heavily on habit, often seen as the antithesis of creativity. However, habits can open up new possibilities for the creative's mind. Suzannah's Olympic training instilled a level of mental toughness that withstood any distractions or glitches, enabling her team to score the first perfect 10s in their sport.

The importance of the mental game is not lost on Suzannah, who noted, 'We did a lot of mental training. We had a coach who worked with us on visualization. I knew what my feet felt like on the deck before I walked out there. I knew what the crowd, energy, and focus would look like. We practiced these things constantly. The final performance was just putting into practice what we'd been training for our whole lives."

For Olympic athletes, the final seconds of a winning performance are the culmination of years and thousands of hours of dedicated practice. Michael Jordan, known for his fierce competitiveness both in games and in practice, famously said that championships are won while the stands are empty. This principle applies to any art form. The mastery of such focus and flexibility originates in the mental arena, where intense practice occurs within the mind long before it is seen by others.

Suzannah recounted a critical moment before the Olympics: "We did a final exhibition for all of our friends and family before the Games. In the first forty seconds, the music cut off. The underwater and above-air speakers jammed, but we were so well trained that we didn't stop. We had prepared to get through any fault. So we just watched each other move and completed the entire routine in silence."

This ability to adapt under pressure is a testament to the rigorous training and mental resilience that elite athletes like Suzannah develop so that they can handle anything that happens in competition. "You've already trained through the hard stuff. That grit is established," she said. "At 6:00 AM, you're at practice, and at 4:00 in the afternoon that same day, you have to go through your routine. You have nothing left, and you hope you can make it through—and you do."

Suzannah also talked about the importance of team dynamics. "In a team performance, you're completely dependent on teammates. You need to have all of the players in sync, all the hard times, all the crying—the real challenges of suffering together, which we all do in this world together."

This cohesion was crucial for Suzannah's team as they prepared for the Atlanta Olympics. She described an intense preparation period: "Coming out to our training facilities two weeks before our event, the focus was on putting things together. Our head coach was keyed in on [our] working together, being healthy and synchronized, but things were not going well. When the coaches realized this, they drove for a couple of hours to Alabama and found a pool, the first thing that was available, and they stuck us there for a week. They knew that we needed to sort ourselves out. At one point, after we'd been there a couple of days, they said, 'You guys need to sit and talk and figure out what's going on, because we've done all the work on the physical.'"

It was essential for Suzannah's team to find their way back to group flow before heading to the Olympics. "It feels like you have eyes in the back of your head, as if you can feel the people behind you," she said. "You don't have to use your eyes. If you could see us in some kind of video that was weighing and measuring energy, we would have the same heart rate. We all were painted with the same color and energy. That's the only way I can visualize that kind of connectedness because we don't have a lot of words for it. I can picture it in my head: you know when you're in sync. You know when you're in the flow. You can feel everyone moving, that glimpse out of the corner of your eye. You're just moving from point A to point B. It's incredible."

This connection and camaraderie among team members were vital. "You have to trust yourself," Suzannah said. "That's a huge part of it because in a group of team members, there's always that flicker of 'What if I mess up? What if I'm the one?' That's a whole different pressure than anyone doing a solo type of event. So there's that added effort, like 'Okay, I can push this farther than I could on my own because I can't let anybody down.' You add that energy to team flow, where you have to give it 100 percent because that's what's required from everyone."

For those gearing up for their first big performance, Suzannah's advice was clear: stick to your established routines and rituals. "I'd say to the first timer that whatever habits you have established for your training and performance regimen, you keep those. You work them into the fabric of how you're getting in there. Any big change will be a detriment because the process of preparing to perform takes time, and one can lose sight because it has a structure. You don't just say, 'Oh,' and all of a sudden, you're on stage and ready to go. There's always a mental step-by-step process. It doesn't matter if you're performing for your parents or at the Olympics; it's essentially the same.

"Keep the habit of your preperformance process—not just for performing as an athlete, but for whatever actions you need to do. The way you get ready, the way you check your bag in the locker room, the shoes you're wearing, all of that is an important part of the process."

Addressing the mental pressures of a big performance, Suzannah advised, "This is a unique performance, but you've done it a hundred or a thousand times, and it's nothing new. All you need to do is the same thing you've always done. What you don't know is the other part, like the sound of the crowd, the roar of fifteen thousand people. That can be a little overwhelming, but mentally, you can prepare for it."

∦ CREATIVE SPARKS 2 ∦

Create "pressure cooker" scenarios in your practice sessions. Simulate real performance conditions or throw in unexpected challenges to build resilience and mental fortitude. What steps can you take to ensure your practice environment equips you for high-pressure situations?

SEEKING INSPIRATION AND CHASING GOALS

Suzannah's disciplined mindset was shaped not only by her rigorous training but also by the inspirations she encountered along the way.

Many kids develop a lifelong passion for sports, drawing, writing, or other forms of creativity. What drives some children to train harder and ultimately excel? For Suzannah, having an older sister involved in synchronized swimming made all the difference.

Suzannah looked up to her and thought, "I want to be that good." She had role models both on the big stage and within her swimming club who were exceptionally skilled. Watching the Olympics cemented her ambition: "That's it. That's my goal. I want to be an Olympic champion."

Suzannah's early success at age ten came more quickly than her sister's, who didn't start excelling until she was fourteen or fifteen. Their parents ensured the girls were at the pool morning, noon, and night, taking care of everything else at home. Suzannah never had to worry about dinner; her mom handled it all, fostering an environment where they could focus entirely on their sport.

The media often tried to create a rivalry between the sisters, but their family didn't encourage that. Instead, competitions were viewed as opportunities. Suzannah felt happy for her sister if she won everything, never adopting an "It should be me" attitude. Her sister's hard work and dedication were clear; she was the first one at the pool and the last one out.

Success often arises from a series of fortuitous events. For Suzannah, synchronized swimming being added as an Olympic sport came at the perfect moment. This timing was akin to how new technologies or market shifts can create opportunities in the arts. Being mentally prepared to seize them is crucial.

"It was on the world stage, but it wasn't in the Olympics until 1984. I joined just before that," Suzannah said. "Then, for the first time, you had these amazing and glamorous athletes that were in the Olympics."

Her team already had a strong familiarity with each other before their Olympic training year, thanks to their preliminary and national competitions. This familiarity helped solidify their teamwork during that crucial year. Each member had a distinct role: a cheerleader, a perfectionist, a rhythm person for timing. This balance made them a well-rounded team.

The rigorous training included a forty-five-minute daily commute they shared. They would ride together, sleep in the car, and fully dedicate themselves to their sport. "We were all in—that was our lives at the time."

⚡ **CREATIVE SPARKS 3** ⚡

Reflect on your early creative influences, whether family, mentors, or cultural events. How did they shape your creative path, and have these influences evolved over time? Analyze how these experiences have molded your creative journey.

TAKING CUES FROM COLLABORATORS

Creativity thrives in solo studios or in team settings like *Saturday Night Live*. Often, collective creation outshines solitary achievements. The best creators acknowledge and express gratitude for their collaborators' vital roles, much as movie credits, with their long list of diverse contributors, highlight the importance of a group coming together.

Suzannah's journey from Olympic champion to Cirque du Soleil performer exemplifies the impact of being surrounded by incredibly talented individuals. Cirque du Soleil's dynamic and supportive collaborators allowed her creativity to flourish, pushed her boundaries, and inspired her to new heights.

"I have a trained eye from synchronized swimming, but at Cirque du Soleil, you are constantly around incredibly talented people," Suzannah reflected. "Technicians could also be trapeze flyers, and you might find the only person in the world who has done five somersaults. Whether they're into metal sculpture or painting, we have incredibly talented people from all over the world."

Each day at Cirque du Soleil revealed a collaborative culture where performers brought unique elements from their respective backgrounds. "Mongolians move differently from Russians, and you don't understand this nuance until you see it. The heart of a culture comes out in a person's personality," Suzannah explained. "Hungarians are bold and strong. The Cantonese have a high level of precision in everything they do. Being with other cultures helps [us] push past personal boundaries and explore new possibilities."

The synergy of working with others sparks unparalleled creativity. "You can wonder out loud, and then someone says, 'We can make that happen. Let's build that apparatus.' You get to explore and bring your ideas to life. The creativity available from working with others is unfathomable," Suzannah declared.

Transitioning from the pinnacle of a sport to a new creative context like Cirque du Soleil posed unique challenges for Suzannah. "All the things necessary for competition aren't needed for performing. You need to get out of your routine," she said. Instead of repeating familiar synchronized swimming techniques, such as pointed feet and tight knee extensions, Suzannah suddenly had to think outside the box and improvise.

This shift allowed for immense creativity. "You have to create your path, which allows for huge creativity because you're no longer limited by what role models say," Suzannah noted. "Our director wanted us to show what our bodies could express, turning that into choreography. It pulls the creativity out of you, removing the limitations of competitive rules."

✶ CREATIVE SPARKS 4 ✶

Think back to a creative group project. How did your teammates' skills and perspectives shape the final outcome? Did this experience alter your approach to teamwork and your creative process? Use these insights to enhance future collaborations.

FROM OLYMPIC GLORY TO CIRQUE DU SOLEIL

Suzannah's Olympic achievements set the stage for her next creative challenge: performing with Cirque du Soleil. Transitioning from an Olympic sport to a world-renowned performance company brought unique changes in both preparation and mindset.

"There's a lot to let go," Suzannah explained. "There's a lot to be said about self-talk. For me, focus is essential. I'm physically an athlete and can mentally visualize. I see myself performing the movement or routine exactly, which greatly impacts how my body responds. That's my first rule: I can be the best in what I need to do."

Her transition from Olympic competition to Cirque du Soleil highlights an athlete's ability to expand focus, moving from pure physical execution to storytelling through movement. This shift requires not only physical skill but also mental adaptability, as Suzannah seamlessly integrates narrative and emotion into her performances.

Visualization played a key role when Suzannah tore her serratus anterior, a muscle along the ribs that reaches up to the upper scapula, which took months to heal. "I couldn't use my arm for about six months. I floated in the water, doing only one position to perfect it mentally. Visualization was vital. Despite the struggle, I started using that arm for figures two weeks before nationals and went from doing nothing to competing in the main competition."

Visualization not only facilitated her recovery but also helped her transition from Olympic training to performing arts, demonstrating mental training's power in overcoming new challenges. "I could see myself executing the routine perfectly, even when I physically couldn't perform," Suzannah said. "This mental practice bridged the gap between injury and performance, underscoring the power of mindset."

The narrative of ex-Olympians' post-competitive careers highlights transition challenges. Elite athletes face personal and professional adjustments, including lost routine and identity, which Suzannah navigated through a new creative pursuit.

What happens to ex-Olympians after their competitive careers end? They are elite athletes but also regular people who need to earn a living, raise a family, and face personal challenges. The transition from intense training to a new life can be daunting, but finding a new creative outlet helped Suzannah navigate this challenge successfully.

"One thing sports associations could improve on is offering psychological support for athletes during transitions," Suzannah said. "After the Olympics, you're focused solely on competition, with no room for 'What's next?' The physical and mental strain of training eight hours a day makes stopping suddenly a shock to the body. Athletes need to manage this hormonal change effectively.

"In Cirque du Soleil, I was used to the physical demands and endorphin highs from performing five nights a week. If that stopped abruptly, it would be hard to maintain those levels. After the Olympics, I had to keep moving to manage my body's endorphins. It's about balancing physical activity and emotional recovery."

Taking time off post-Olympics was essential, but she also needed to stay active. "Working at a clinic and coaching helped me stay connected to my sport. One of my former students even joined Cirque du Soleil, which was a wonderful gift."

"When Cirque du Soleil called, I was hesitant but intrigued," she recalled. "I went to Santa Monica for an audition, learning a dance routine from a choreographer. This marked the start of a new journey, blending my athletic background with a new creative pursuit."

⚡ CREATIVE SPARKS 5 ⚡

As you finish a project, identify what you'll miss most—whether it's the thrill of problem-solving, the rush of performing, or the sense of community. Find ways to incorporate these elements into your next endeavor. This will keep you focused, motivated, and inspired, ensuring your creative joy continues through transitions and challenges.

FINDING A CREATIVE X FACTOR

Transitioning between high-performance arenas, Suzannah discovered new dimensions of creativity. While this is personal, it often flourishes in a collective environment. There's a unique thrill in being part of something larger. Scientists note that joining a "virtual large mind" separates humans from animals, enabling us to grow by working together toward a common goal. This synergy connects creators with their audience, creating a shared experience.

"The crowd's energy is invaluable," Suzannah said. "I read an article about tests where they put heart rate monitors on performers and the audience. They found that during certain parts of the performance, the heart rates synced up. I feel that when the heart rate syncs with the audience, you can sense all that tension coming. When the audience is small, you don't feel the same round of applause or energy pushing back at you on the stage."

It's important that rehearsals mirror what the audience ends up seeing. "When we train, I train as if we're performing. There's a part where we're smiling, and when we're up there, that's how I train because I can't do it another way now. My body has been trained to smile while performing. I put myself into that energy state every time, and it is rewarded."

She also shared an inspiring story about the intrinsic rewards of performing for passion rather than primarily for money. "I once heard about a cyclist who performed and was given flowers. I've often thought that if money wasn't involved and I didn't need it to live, I would absolutely perform for flowers. That would be just as good."

As much as Suzannah's dual careers have honed her physical skills, her mental game has been equally vital in her success. Whether competing in the pool or performing to sell-out audiences on stage, her elite mindset has set Suzannah apart.

"When I think of creativity and a creative's mind, there are physical and mental aspects," she said. "One is to enjoy what you do and know that inspiration can be found everywhere. There's nowhere uninteresting when you're in a creative state. If you can't find something interesting or inspiring—like watching drops of water form at the side of a fountain and make ripples—then you're not in the proper mindset. There's no shortage of source material for creativity."

She highlighted the qualities Cirque du Soleil seeks. "As a performer, if you're auditioning for Cirque du Soleil, you have to know the part, give it everything you've got, and be bigger, bolder, and more because that's what Cirque du Soleil is looking for. There are tons of people with fantastic gymnastic skills, but if you don't have that something extra, it's not going to make you stand out. What will make you stand out is going big, above and beyond. Don't be afraid to crawl out of your comfort zone and explode out the top."

Suzannah Bianco's journey from Olympic glory to Cirque du Soleil exemplifies the power of persistence, creativity, and mental fortitude. Her story inspires us to embrace our passions, remain resilient through challenges, and continuously seek new growth avenues. By finding joy in both the routine and the extraordinary, Suzannah reminds us that true fulfillment comes from a deep love for what we do and the relentless pursuit of our dreams.

⚡ CREATIVE SPARKS 6 ⚡

Recall a moment when you felt deeply connected with others during a creative process. How did this shared energy elevate your work? Reflect on how to tap into this collective synergy in future projects to boost your creativity and amplify your impact.

THE 5 Cs IN SUZANNAH BIANCO'S JOURNEY

Suzannah Bianco's journey from Olympic synchronized swimming to Cirque du Soleil exemplifies the principles of mental toughness through the 5 Cs:

1. **Courage:** Suzannah demonstrated immense courage in transitioning from Olympic swimming to performing with Cirque du Soleil. Her willingness to embrace new challenges and adapt to diverse environments highlights her bravery.
2. **Confidence:** Suzannah's confidence was bolstered by visualizing success, from perfect swimming routines to flawless stage

performances. These mental rehearsals strengthened her self-belief and set the stage for her achievements.

3. **Concentration:** With disciplined training in both sports and performing arts, Suzannah's intense focus on perfecting every routine exemplifies her exceptional concentration. This focus ensures her performances are consistently impeccable.

4. **Composure:** Suzannah navigated the pressures of competitions and live performances by employing gratitude and mindful breathing techniques. These strategies allowed her to remain composed and perform with elegance, even under intense stress.

5. **Commitment:** Suzannah's commitment to excellence is evident in her ongoing rigorous training and continuous skill development. Her dedication drives her success, from Olympic competitions to captivating performances at Cirque du Soleil.

YOUR CREATIVE TOOLKIT

Just as Suzannah Bianco exemplifies the 5 Cs of mental toughness in her journey as an Olympic gold medalist and Cirque du Soleil performer, you too can develop these strengths. Here are practical tips and tools based on the 5 Cs of creativity, inspired by her journey.

1. **Courage:**
   - **Rise Above Setbacks:** Setbacks are inevitable but they don't define you. Each "no" offers valuable lessons. Analyze what went wrong, revise your strategy, and keep moving forward. Every rejection brings you closer to the "yes" you deserve.
   - **Transform Doubt into Drive:** True courage isn't about being fearless but about pushing forward despite anxieties. Embrace the challenges and uncertainties of creating. Let them drive you to refine your skills and pursue your goals with determination.
   - **Unleash Your Inner Trailblazer:** Don't shy away from experimentation and risk-taking. Share your unique vision

with the world. The art community needs your fresh perspective and innovative ideas!

2. **Confidence:**

- **Embrace Your Principles:** Build self-respect by consistently aligning your actions with your core principles. Let integrity guide the authenticity of your work, and embrace continual learning and growth to enhance your skills. This alignment fosters a deep sense of fulfillment and direction in your creative endeavors. Repeat after me: "I trust my principles to guide my creative journey, and I commit to living them fully."

- **Cultivate Self-Acceptance:** Focus on self-acceptance to fully embrace all aspects of your being—strengths, challenges, and unique quirks. This acceptance enriches your perspective, boosting your confidence and empowering you to express your creativity with authenticity. Remind yourself: "I embrace my authentic self, celebrating my unique strengths, challenges, and creative spirit."

- **Trust Your Worth:** Recognize that your worth as a creative is intrinsic and not contingent on external recognition or successes. Trust in your artistic abilities and value your creative contributions as inherently significant. This internal assurance allows you to navigate the creative process with confidence and resilience. Remind yourself: "I am enough, and my creative worth is unconditional—I trust myself to create with purpose and passion."

3. **Concentration:**

- **Energize for Creativity:** Long hours don't equal better art. Prioritize self-care to recharge your energy: get quality sleep, eat nutritious meals, and exercise regularly. A healthy body fuels the focus needed to bring your vision to life.

- **Take Creative Breaks:** Short breaks can boost creativity. Schedule them regularly to maintain focus. Step away from your project, take a walk, or do some stretches. Returning with fresh eyes can lead to unexpected solutions and creative breakthroughs.

- **Build Creative Endurance:** Creative focus is a marathon, not a sprint. Replenish your physical and mental reserves with activities like meditation, spending time with loved ones, or enjoying a relaxing hobby. These practices help you return to your work with renewed energy and inspiration.

4. **Composure:**
   - **Breathe Your Way to Calm:** Learn the 4-7-8 breathing technique to effectively manage stress and anxiety. This simple yet powerful method involves inhaling for four seconds, holding for seven, and exhaling for eight, activating your body's natural relaxation response.
   - **Establish a Daily Calming Routine:** Practice the 4-7-8 technique consistently and patiently for just two to five minutes each day, ideally at the same time and place, such as first thing in the morning or right before your creative sessions.
   - **Unlock Resilience Under Pressure:** As you master the 4-7-8 technique, it becomes a powerful tool for building resilience and navigating creative challenges with confidence, clarity, and poise.

5. **Commitment:**
   - **Ignite Your Vision:** Craft a vision board that sparks your creative spirit. Fill it with images, quotes, and representations of your goals. Let this visual roadmap ignite your dreams and fuel your passion.
   - **Keep Your Vision Fresh:** Keep your vision board fresh by regularly updating it to reflect your evolving goals and aspirations. Let your board evolve with you as you pursue new challenges.
   - **Make It a Daily Motivator:** Your vision board isn't just a decoration—it's a powerful tool. This constant visual reminder keeps your commitment to achieving your dreams at the forefront of your mind. Let it inspire you to take action and persevere on your journey. Where will you display your vision board?

IN THE NEXT CHAPTER

Imagination meets perseverance in the inspiring story of Tim Allen, a visionary animator who transformed his childhood passion into a ground-breaking career. Join Tim on his captivating journey, exploring how his innovative spirit, relentless drive for excellence, and distinctive creative vision have propelled him to the forefront of the animation industry.

Chapter 6

ONE FRAME AT A TIME: TIM ALLEN

This is the strangest dinner party imaginable. One guest is a hunchback; another has a round head far too large for his puny body. Four wear top hats almost as tall as they are. The host's face is pallid, as white as a ghost. Beside him sits his reluctant bride, looking as though she stepped straight out of a horror movie. And she did, because this isn't a real gathering; it's a scene from Tim Burton's Corpse Bride. At one end of the table, a shaven-headed Brit looms over the oddball figures like a giant. He makes a minute adjustment to a character's hair, then takes a couple of pictures. Adjust. Position. Shoot. This precision and eye for detail have earned this animator's films two Academy Awards.

The debate over whether creativity is nature or nurture may never be resolved. Growing up in 1970s England, Tim Allen and his sister benefited from both. "You couldn't stop me drawing when I was a child, and I loved playing with action figures," Tim said. "I recently found some photos for my sister's wedding and was reminded just how many creative things my mum got us involved in, whether it was LEGO competitions, sending cartoons to the local newspaper, or getting us in the annual carnival.

Anytime there were costumes involved, she made them herself. I always had a lot of energy and would say I'm a doer—I have to make things."

His parents' divorce cast a dark shadow over these happy times and his budding creativity. When he was sixteen, Tim needed to decide on the next steps in his education but found it hard to figure out who he was and what kind of career he wanted to pursue. During this time he faced a pivotal moment that would shape his future, discovered his true passion, and started a journey that led him to the world of animation.

FINDING PURPOSE IN MOTION

Tim was at a crossroads, grappling with personal turmoil and a lack of clear direction. "At that stage I was very lost, and it wasn't just to do with personal things like my parents' marriage breaking down and the life I knew being shattered," Tim said. "I'm sure that added to it, but in terms of my direction as a creative professional, I had no idea, and I definitely hadn't found my thing."

Seeking clarity, Tim explored various creative disciplines, enrolling in a four-module course that covered fashion, calligraphy, three-dimensional design, and fine arts. His interest in anatomy and motion initially drew him toward animatronics and model making. However, a chance encounter changed everything. "I went to a university to look at a model-making degree and while I was waiting, someone said, 'Is anyone here to see the animation course?' It hadn't dawned on me that you could do that in college or as a job," Tim explained. "That lit me up because I realized I'd found my thing."

Tim's childhood love for animation, fueled by classics like *The Wind in the Willows*, *Fireman Sam*, and *Postman Pat*, found new purpose with the release of *The Nightmare Before Christmas*. "It was my favorite film. I bought a book about the making of it, but I'd never joined the dots and recognized that this was a career I could go for. Suddenly, I'd found my purpose in life," Tim said.

Despite *The Nightmare Before Christmas* raising the profile of animation and Aardman's Oscar-winning *Wallace and Gromit* films, the UK had limited educational opportunities in this field. Tim evaluated the few available courses and decided that Cardiff University in Wales offered the best setting and syllabus for his aspirations.

Once enrolled, Tim felt at home but soon faced a harsh reality check. His first major project evaluation was brutal. "We had a critique where the tutor looked at our work in front of the whole class and gave us his feedback," Tim recounted. "He ripped the shit out of me in front of the rest of the class, and I was shamed in front of everyone. He said my animation and model making were rubbish, which I disagreed with."

This tough critique became a turning point for Tim, fueling his determination to improve and excel in the field of animation.

⚡ CREATIVE SPARKS 1 ⚡

Revisit the creative activities that brought you joy as a child—whether it's play, drawing, building, or imagining. Keep a "creative journal" to capture ideas and insights, using a notebook, app, or sketchbook. Watch your curiosity and creativity flourish!

BECOMING A SPECIALIST

With a newfound sense of direction, Tim plunged into the world of animation. His relentless pursuit of mastery underscores the dedication and resilience required to excel in his chosen field. In fact, Tim's journey stands as a testament to the value of deep specialization, challenging the notion that pursuing a singular aim can lead to an unhealthy obsession.

While society often promotes balance and generalism (the practice of having a broad range of skills), Tim's dedication to mastering his craft exemplifies the power of fixating on one thing. He advises budding animators to seek knowledge and fully immerse themselves in their passion by learning as much as possible and engaging with industry veterans.

"Be an information sponge," Tim said. "If you're fascinated by something, learn all about it. Watch YouTube videos, study careers and techniques. When you meet people at film festivals, you'll ask better questions if you understand the industry landscape. Put yourself out there."

Tim underscored the value of posing straightforward, insightful questions when interacting with professionals. "Instead of being anxious, say something like 'Please tell me how you started' or 'Tell me your story.' Ask, 'What did you find difficult?' Seek information rather than trying to prove what you've learned."

Not every interaction will go smoothly. Tim shared a humorous, somewhat embarrassing memory from the first Cardiff Animation Festival, where he got drunk in front of Peter Lord, co-founder of Aardman. Despite the mishap, it fueled his determination to improve his skills. "Seeing professional productions made me realize the level I needed to reach," Tim said. "I wasn't there yet, and that made me frustrated because I'm a perfectionist. But it motivated me to double down on my projects."

Tim's resolve led to producing a high-quality second-year film, and he later embraced valuable real-world advice from his instructor. "Chris's words of wisdom stayed with me: get companies to know your name, don't burn bridges, and treat people well. We're all victims of our personalities; strengths in one situation can be damaging in another."

After completing his degree, Tim was determined to work full time in animation, but had to pay his dues first. He attended festivals, networked, and shared his portfolio while working at a local rec center. This experience taught him adaptability and the importance of a work ethic.

"I did various jobs, from lifeguarding to selling ice cream. I learned how to be reliable and do my best in everything," Tim said. "In my spare time, I continued to put my name and work out to potential employers. You have to recognize that nineteen out of twenty opportunities aren't going to lead to anything. But that's okay. As long as you're out there meeting people and getting involved, that one thing will become something more."

Tim faced rejection from every animation company in the UK, but persevered. "I told myself, 'They're not ready for me yet,' and kept meeting people. After eighteen months, I started getting practical work experience, including test animations on the set of *Bob the Builder*."

Building relationships over time, Tim approached pivotal people at companies with humility and offered to pitch in with menial tasks. "One director needed help moving his studio, not animating. I decided that it would be interesting to see some of the puppets, props, and everything else they were cleaning out of the cupboards. So I packed up loads of boxes and put them in a truck. The next time there was animation work, he hired me."

For Tim, mastery required not just singular dedication but also patience and the willingness to take on any opportunity to get a foot in the door. By fusing creativity, determination, and purpose, he was on the road to realizing his dreams.

✍ CREATIVE SPARKS 2 ✍

Choose a creative pursuit that excites you and set specific, achievable goals. Attack these aims with relentless commitment. Whether it's taking a course or dedicating hours to practice, consistent effort and unwavering focus lead to profound growth.

As Tim honed his skills, he quickly realized the importance of learning from those who had walked the path before him. He built valuable relationships with mentors who shaped his career and provided invaluable guidance.

Imagine being a soccer player with Lionel Messi or Alex Morgan posters adorning your bedroom wall and one day, many years later, getting the opportunity to play alongside them. This was the kind of delight Tim experienced when he received a call to audition for *Corpse Bride*, produced by the same visionary behind his favorite film, *The Nightmare Before Christmas*: Tim Burton. Upon securing the role, Tim Allen was determined that his work on *Corpse Bride* wouldn't just be a noteworthy addition to his CV. He was also eager to absorb everything he could from the talented animators he would work alongside for the next several months.

"The one I got to know best was Anthony Scott," Tim said. "He was the supervisor, and a lovely, sweet guy. Years later we saw each other for the first time in seventeen years on the *Pinocchio* set, which was really cool, as I was just a young twenty-seven-year-old when I first met him on *Corpse Bride*. Anthony was the first guy who went through my work frame by frame, pointing out a lot of my inconsistencies."

Tim reminisced about how Anthony had been the same age on *The Nightmare Before Christmas* as Tim was on *Corpse Bride*. It was fascinating for Tim to reflect on their parallel journeys and how their careers had evolved. "At the same age, we both worked on our first feature film, and it was a Tim Burton one."

Another mentor Tim found invaluable was Mike Johnson, the animation director on *Corpse Bride* who also animated *The Nightmare Before Christmas*. Although they didn't work as closely as Tim and Anthony, their conversations at the pub after work were enlightening. Mike was very open about the ups and downs of his career, and Tim found solace in realizing that these accomplished animators were just regular people who had started a decade or so before him. This perspective was grounding and inspiring for Tim, knowing he could one day be in a similar position.

⁄ CREATIVE SPARKS 3 ⁄

Reflect on a pivotal mentor, parent, or teacher. What's the most impactful advice they've shared, and how has it shaped your creative approach? Broaden your insights further by asking peers about the guidance that has been influential in their own work.

PLAYING A LONG GAME

In a world where quick wins are immediately shared on social media platforms, it can be difficult for less experienced creators to realize that such stills and video highlights capture less than one percent of the legwork that goes into true craftsmanship. Tim emphasized this point by sharing an example from his feature-length work.

"One of the longest marathon scenes I've done was for *Corpse Bride*," Tim said. "Barkis is at the very end of the table, and the camera's tracking along it. All the guests are looking super bored as the shot slowly moves toward him. It took a week for rehearsals and then four more weeks to shoot the whole thing. Every day was very similar to the one before, just tracking down a vanishing point with microscopic movements."

Despite the monotony, Tim found ways to stay motivated. "I tried to be a bit Zen about stuff like that and keep track of the number of frames I did. I had to report to production how I was doing each day and was able to quantify it. Seeing that number be a bit higher and giving myself little challenges each day, like getting to a certain point by a certain time, helped."

Tim also made sure to prioritize his mental health during these long film shoots. "It's very easy to get cabin fever when you're in the same room doing similar things, working long days, and even coming in on Saturdays," Tim said. "You need to create mental space, even if that's just by getting outside and taking a long walk at lunchtime. Looking out to sea or at nature—whether you're outside or just by a window—will make your brain produce more serotonin."

He explained the physical and mental benefits of such breaks. "If you're hunched over a laptop all day, your cortisol goes up and it's stressful. It's also going to release dopamine if you can do some breathing exercises where you open up your diaphragm and get a decent amount of oxygen in."

By taking these small but significant steps, Tim ensures he can maintain his well-being and continue to bring his best to every project. Balancing work with self-care was key to his sustained creativity and success.

⚡ **CREATIVE SPARKS 4** ⚡

Rate how well you prioritize mental health during long projects (1 = low, 5 = high). Are you taking breaks, staying active, and managing stress? Identify areas for improvement and add a new habit like breaks or meditation. Ensure you have a go-to person for support. Set an intention to prioritize mental health in your next project.

NAVIGATING POST-SUCCESS BLUES

Following the success of *Corpse Bride*, which built on techniques pioneered during *The Nightmare Before Christmas* and secured its place among classic animated features, Tim faced a new challenge. While he welcomed the chance to elevate his game and relished the success of this seminal film, he had to combat the "arrival fallacy," a concept described by Harvard professor Tal Ben-Shahar as the false belief that achieving a goal will bring ultimate satisfaction.

"I had just about enough experience to rise to the challenge on *Corpse*," Tim said. "There's an expectation these days of things happening quickly, but success is short-lived. I've got friends who've won Oscars, and I've worked on two films that have won them. It's meant to be the best moment of your life, but it's just a moment. There will be times when it works out and others when it doesn't. Success doesn't eliminate anxieties. Once you climb a mountain, you need another goal."

Many creators encounter post-project blues, feeling directionless after achieving significant success. *Corpse Bride* earned $118 million, received critical acclaim, and was nominated for an Academy Award. However, Tim witnessed some animators becoming complacent, which illustrated to him the importance of continuously setting new goals to maintain motivation and drive.

"Some animators thought they'd never do children's TV again, but

I knew that was unrealistic. Within weeks, I was back on the set of *Fifi and the Flowertots*. It wasn't glamorous, but it was work. Some animators didn't do anything for months and blew through their savings. [The actor] Michael Caine said he'd always take the best available role, meaning you go from big projects to small ones because prestigious gigs aren't always available. If you think you've reached the top, you might find there's nothing out there."

After returning to TV work, Tim's perseverance paid off when Aardman recognized his talents. While working with Aardman's team, including creative director Merlin Crossingham, he came across the next challenge: "The feeling was, 'Okay, you can animate, but can you sculpt?'" In response, he adopted a growth mindset. "I went in with an open mind, ready to learn their techniques. I didn't have a *Corpse Bride* ego. I wanted to be the best Aardman animator I could be. I had to become an information sponge all over again."

Working with Aardman repeatedly allowed Tim to spend time with an industry legend who was the animation director on *Who Framed Roger Rabbit* and influenced him early in his career. "One day, I saw Richard Williams at Aardman. They'd given him his own studio after he retired. I'd met him before at a film festival, but now I could go to him almost as a student. We'd discuss frame-by-frame decisions and shooting in 3D."

Tim's ability to navigate the highs and lows of his career as he transitioned between projects, big or small, was in large part due to his eagerness to seek out challenges with a growth mindset—critical to success and creative satisfaction in any industry as dynamic as animation.

⚲ CREATIVE SPARKS 5 ⚲

After completing a project or hitting a milestone, don't stop. Push your creativity by trying something new—like a painter experimenting with sculpture or a writer exploring a different genre. Keep your momentum going by always seeking the next challenge.

ADOPTING CREATIVE FLEXIBILITY

When a creator reaches the level of Tim Allen, it might be easy to play it safe within a single form. Not Tim. When asked to contribute to Wes Anderson's first feature-length animation, *Fantastic Mr. Fox*, he was reminded of the need to adapt and wear several different hats. "I tried to do the Wes Anderson style on *Fox* and my first tests weren't there at all," Tim recalled. "It was Wes's vision, and we were there to give him what he wanted. Wes is very focused on certain details and long, lingering shots. I was there at the end of the film, doing bits and bobs; whatever shots were left. The most challenging shot was animating two hundred chickens behind Mr. Fox in a barn. I had to learn to adapt to new styles very quickly."

The stellar work of the animators under Anderson's direction and the exemplary voice acting performances of George Clooney, Meryl Streep, and Bill Murray resonated with audiences and critics. *Fantastic Mr. Fox* earned nominations at the Academy Awards, Golden Globes, and the BAFTAs. So it was no surprise when Anderson's team brought Tim back for their next animated project, *Isle of Dogs*. Animating the villains—Mayor Kobayashi and Major Domo—allowed Tim to shoot some of his most amusing scenes to date and reminded him that while his role requires precision, it doesn't demand perfection.

When discussing his work, Tim shares his experiences with humility. "When I do presentations in workshops or at festivals, I love to show mistakes I've made in films," he said. "For example, in *Isle of Dogs*, where the mayor gets out of the bathtub and you see his naked bottom, I didn't have him quite high enough, and Wes wanted more crevice between his butt cheeks. This is an ongoing journey. I'm not a 'master of stop motion' as it says on the poster. I'm a guy who's figuring it out and getting certain things right and others wrong as I go."

One reason Tim makes such changes seamlessly is that he continually participates in projects that challenge him and works with experts in other techniques. "Where's the next thing that I don't know that much about and could do with improving?" Tim asked himself. "Where's the new opportunity and challenge? While working with Mark [James Roles] and Emma [de Swaef] on *The House*, it was using felt. To give the puppets' faces a bit of extra stretch, I got impatient and started dipping a brush in hot water and rubbing it on. Soon they started streaking. Emma showed me how she uses steam instead. It takes longer, but there's no streaking."

For many years, Tim would have found such challenges daunting, but now he embraces them. "That's something I don't know how to do. Great. Let's figure it out. If I stay at the same place doing very similar stuff all the time, I'm going to get bored and bitter. I have a hunger to learn and need to see progression."

After completing back-to-back projects for Wes Anderson, Tim turned to more TV work. Then he got a call for one of the most ambitious animated films to date: *Pinocchio*, a remake of the classic Disney original. The film enabled Tim to focus on a single project for eight months rather than juggling several. "At Aardman, the style is much more poppy and cartoony, whereas *Pinocchio* had more of a hyperrealistic style," Tim said. "I got to work with Anthony Scott again, seventeen years after we'd first teamed up on *Corpse Bride*. I had to put my life on hold to be there. It was Guillermo del Toro's first animation, a great team, and I'd already seen the stunning sculptures from Mackinnon & Saunders, the puppet makers in Manchester."

"You never get to see the script until after you get on set," Tim added. "The Zoom interview was very direct—basically, 'These are the terms and conditions. Do you accept them? This is how the pay structure works. Are you in?' It was an easy decision creatively and beneficial for my career long term."

Filming *Pinocchio* meant being thousands of miles away from his London home for eight months. The project was creatively satisfying but presented a formidable mindset challenge. "I really struggle with routine anxiety when I'm doing the same thing every day," Tim said. "I like to have different stimuli and give myself little treats, which means eating a lot of cookies! It could also be listening to a podcast episode or having a glass of wine in the evening. There has to be a healthy balance because otherwise, you can fall into a habit of self-punishment."

Tim's instincts to participate in *Pinocchio* proved correct. The project pushed him creatively, and the outcome was remarkable. *Pinocchio* won Best Animated Feature at the 95th Academy Awards, becoming the second Oscar-winning film Tim has animated. He sometimes pursues a more simplistic approach for evaluating such opportunities and uses positive self-talk to stay motivated.

"I remember something Ricky Gervais commented on when he says 'yes' to something: he's not really working because he's doing what he enjoys. I always remind myself, 'Tim, you're here because you love this.' If I feel too exhausted to do a talk or host a workshop, I'll say in my head, 'Just have fun. No one will know if it doesn't go according to plan. Just let your hair down and see what happens.' If you have a smile on your face, it's contagious. I've learned to stop worrying about everything being perfect and now just go with the flow."

Tim's willingness to adapt and embrace new styles, be creatively flexible, and learn continuously not only played a crucial role in his early and mid-career success but have also been key to his sustained progress in the animation industry.

✎ CREATIVE SPARKS 6 ✎

Reflect on a recent project where you had to adapt—like learning new software or changing your style. Note how this led to fresh ideas. For your next project, deliberately choose an unfamiliar approach to keep growing through flexibility and innovation.

SETTING BOUNDARIES AND LEAVING A LEGACY

With a wealth of experience and numerous accolades, Tim's focus shifted toward making a lasting impact. He felt a calling to mentor the next generation of animators, but first he had to learn to balance his professional commitments with teaching.

For his mental well-being, Tim learned to turn down opportunities more often during and after his work on *Pinocchio*. While he enjoys teaching animation students, delivering talks, and replying to inquiries, he realized he couldn't agree to everything. "While I was away in Portland, I had to say no to a lot of requests," Tim said. "I justified it by reminding people that I was busy being a senior animator on Guillermo del Toro's *Pinocchio* and asking them to try again in June. That led to a backlog of people asking for my time. If I said yes to all those things, I wouldn't have any time left at all."

At one point Tim was on the verge of a nervous breakdown from constantly running on adrenaline, traveling to Bristol to work with Aardman on *Chicken Run 2*, mentoring in the evenings, trying to see friends, and fitting in exercise. "The moment I'm not animating, I'm trying to catch up on messages and emails. You can't run on adrenaline all the time. Our bodies and brains need rest. I know myself well enough to recognize when there are malfunctions. Listening to audiobooks on this topic helped me pull back from burnout. I've become reflective and nonjudgmental enough to recognize patterns of behavior and stop myself from getting into the same situation again."

Tim values sharing knowledge with young filmmakers, viewing them as future colleagues and potential employers. He perpetuates the lessons he learned from his mentors by sharing them in workshops. "The next generation is part of the process," Tim said. "They're not here to take my job. These will be my colleagues moving forward and might even be my employer or boss. Many of my students have become world-class animators working at Aardman on *Chicken Run 2* and *Wallace and Gromit*."

Tim's experiences with anxiety and his deep understanding of how the human mind processes fear have made him more self-aware and innovative in his teaching. "I recognize anxiety in my students and their fear of making mistakes," Tim said. "I started reframing right and wrong as more and less effective and introduced calming methods. One exercise—the open, close, or clench stretch—helps people see their body as one entity. Whether we feel safe and happy or insecure and cautious affects our movements. I use these simple philosophies to help students animate a stop-motion puppet as one whole entity."

It's important to Tim to have judgment-free discussions about people's animations. "I create a relaxed, safe, nurturing environment where these conversations are healthy and progressive. We destigmatize mistakes by looking for as many as possible without judging them. I give analogies like getting your porridge too hot or too cold to show the need for a middle ground. I try to help students shed the fear of failure early on so we can focus on better creative decision-making."

Tim's teaching extends beyond formal settings to helping younger colleagues feel welcome and safe in the workplace. "My amygdala has learned that coming into a new situation as an outsider is not so scary because I've done it hundreds of times, didn't die, and didn't get rejected," Tim said. "But I remember being very socially anxious in my early days. That's why I'm keen to put newcomers at ease and give them pointers without being critical. I'm happy to be a friendly face, and many people remember that I was nice to them when they were nervous."

Due to his work on high-profile films and TV shows and his stellar reputation within the industry, Tim receives many requests for career advice. He believes in freely passing on what he's learned and celebrating the successes of others. "I've been teaching for twenty years," Tim said. "I'm grateful to have seen many people's careers begin, struggle, prosper, and grow. Now they're established with families, and I remember them as young students seeking advice. My legacy will be as much about the talks and teaching as it is about the films, in terms of personal connections and the effect I've had on people."

⚡ CREATIVE SPARKS 7 ⚡

Take control of your workload by identifying where you can set realistic boundaries. Learn to say no without guilt, delegate tasks confidently, and prioritize commitments that align with your goals. By doing so, you'll prevent burnout, free up creative energy, and maintain a sustainable balance between work and play.

THE 5 Cs IN TIM ALLEN'S JOURNEY

Tim Allen's journey from a budding animator to an Oscar-winning professional exemplifies the principles of mental toughness through the 5 Cs:

1. **Courage:** Tim demonstrated courage by using early career critiques as motivation to improve, rather than reasons to quit. His bravery is further shown by his willingness to tackle challenging projects like *Corpse Bride* and *Fantastic Mr. Fox*, pushing beyond his comfort zone to master new animation styles.

2. **Confidence:** Collaborating with industry leaders on *Corpse Bride* bolstered Tim's confidence. Mentorship from Anthony Scott and Mike Johnson, combined with his successful handling of intricate scenes, solidified his belief in his abilities and prepared him for increasingly complex projects.

3. **Concentration:** Tim's legendary concentration was crucial during detailed projects. His focused work on *Corpse Bride*, particularly the marathon scene, highlights his meticulous attention to detail and his ability to maintain high standards under intense focus.

4. **Composure:** Keeping his composure under pressure was key to Tim's success, especially in high-stakes projects like *Pinocchio*. By integrating self-care practices like walks and podcasts into his routine, he managed stress effectively, ensuring sustained creativity and mental health.

5. **Commitment:** Tim's deep commitment to animation is shown by his continuous pursuit of knowledge and his willingness to teach others. Despite facing setbacks, his dedication to refining his skills and exploring new challenges exemplifies his relentless drive and commitment to the art of animation.

YOUR CREATIVE TOOLKIT

Just as Tim Allen exemplifies the 5 Cs of creativity through his remarkable career as one of the world's leading stop-motion animators, you too can develop these strengths. Here are practical tips and tools based on the 5 Cs of creativity, inspired by his journey.

1. **Courage:**
   - **Live Your Core Values:** Embrace your unique values by prioritizing authenticity over conformity. Identify and consistently live by your top three core values, such as Authenticity, Curiosity, and Resilience. Use them as a compass to stay true to yourself and your purpose.
   - **Navigate Change Boldly:** Accept change as a constant and adjust your approach when needed. Courageously reflect on your journey to ensure it aligns with your long-term goals. Dedicate time each week to reflect and stay on track.
   - **Turn Setbacks into Springboards:** View setbacks as learning opportunities and springboards for growth, not failures. Each misstep offers a chance to sharpen your skills. Reflect on a recent challenge and identify three ways it has propelled you forward. For example, a musician struggling to master a piece might rewrite it, creating a whole new melody.

2. **Confidence:**
   - **Cultivate Faith in Yourself:** It's easy to have faith and discipline when you're thriving. The real strength lies in believing in yourself and staying focused when success isn't immediate. Set small improvement goals and trust the process, knowing that each step brings you closer. Reflect: How can I maintain self-belief and discipline, even when the results aren't visible yet?
   - **Unlock Your Inner Champion:** Turn your inner dialogue into a powerful cheerleader that fuels your confidence and creativity. Replace self-doubt with affirmations like "I am a creative force" or "I am capable of achieving my dreams." Repeat these mantras daily, especially when you need a boost. Over time, this practice will rewire your mind with positivity, helping you tackle challenges with courage and confidence.

- **Blast Off to Future Success:** Imagine basking in the thrill of wild success—you've crushed your goals and feel like a rockstar. Now visualize the journey that got you here. What steps did you take? What obstacles did you overcome? Replay this mental movie, feeling the pride of your accomplishments. Let this vision inspire bold action and make your dreams a reality!

3. **Concentration:**
   - **Take Mindful Breathing Breaks:** Pause and take three to four mindful nasal breaths immediately before and after you drive or walk somewhere. This practice helps you stay present and grounded, preventing the rush from one place to another. These mindful moments create a sense of calm and enhance your focus throughout the day.
   - **Eliminate Distractions:** Identify what distracts you from your goals and implement strategies to minimize these distractions. Use a timer to work in focused intervals and take short breaks to stay productive without burning out. Create a distraction-free workspace to enhance your focus.
   - **Align Tasks with Goals:** Kick off each week by choosing your top three "big win" tasks that move you closer to your creative dreams. Think of it as creating your personal to-do list for success! By focusing on what really matters, you'll stay on track and make steady progress toward your vision, one step at a time.

4. **Composure:**
   - **Reframe Negative Thoughts:** Notice when negative thoughts arise, such as "I'm not good enough," or "I'll never succeed." Challenge them with more balanced perspectives, like "I've faced challenges before and can learn from them" or "Success is a journey, not a destination." With regular practice, this technique can help you develop a more realistic and encouraging mindset, reducing anxiety and self-doubt over time.
   - **Adjust Behaviors:** Align your behaviors with a positive

interpretation of anxiety. Approach activities with enthusiasm and anticipation rather than dread, reinforcing this reappraisal. This conscious shift in behavior helps you condition yourself to manage anxiety with greater composure.

- **Maintain a Daily Social Practice:** Implement the "smile and hello" technique each day. Make eye contact, smile, and greet at least five new people daily. This simple practice helps reduce social anxiety and build confidence. By making this a habit, you'll develop a more composed and approachable demeanor, making social interactions more enjoyable and less stressful.

5. **Commitment:**
   - **Align Your Daily Routine:** Allocate dedicated time each day to activities that support your long-term goals. Consistency is the bedrock of lasting progress. For example, if you're a painter, reserve an hour each morning for uninterrupted studio time. Use a calendar or planner to schedule this period and treat it as a nonnegotiable commitment.
   - **Be Greater Than Yesterday:** Strive for daily improvement by setting the goal to be better today than you were yesterday. Reflect each evening on your progress and identify one thing you can do better tomorrow. This constant pursuit of growth keeps you moving forward and enhances your commitment to your craft.
   - **Establish Accountability:** Create strong accountability mechanisms such as mentor check-ins or self-assessments. Partner with a reliable colleague or mentor for regular progress reviews. For instance, if you're a musician, arrange biweekly meetings with a mentor to review your practice sessions, discuss challenges, and set goals. This keeps you committed and ensures you stay on track.

IN THE NEXT CHAPTER

Artistry meets innovation in the story of David Greusel, a visionary architect behind iconic designs. Step into his world, where imagination converges with precision, and discover the timeless impact of his ground-breaking structures. Join us on a journey into the creative genius of a true architectural pioneer.

Chapter 7

ARCHITECT OF DREAMS: DAVID GREUSEL

The architect adjusts his black-rimmed glasses, picks up his fine-tipped pencil, and leans over his tilted drafting table, ready to start drawing. He unrolls a large sheet of paper like a medieval scroll, pauses momentarily, and then begins to draw. This will become the blueprint for an award-winning Major League Baseball ballpark, but for now all that matters is putting down the first lines to get his mind and the ambitious project going. After a few hours, he has sketched the outline of the building's north elevation. Smiling, he steps back, satisfied, knowing he's laid the foundation for the finer details yet to come.

Major League Baseball parks are highly utilitarian, designed to accommodate thousands of spectators who need to sit, move, eat, and use the facilities. Any breakdown in these functions can impact the experience and the vitality of the game. With fans' passions at stake and millions invested by developers and cities, the burden on an architect can be heavy.

David Greusel, FAIA, an architect with more than thirty years of experience, understands these challenges deeply. As the lead designer for PNC Park (home of the Pittsburgh Pirates) and Minute Maid Park (home of the Houston Astros), Greusel has tackled these complexities head-on. His career includes roles as principal and shareholder in large and medium-sized architectural firms across the Midwest, with responsibilities spanning every aspect of architectural project delivery, including design, programming, planning, and project management.

TAKING BOLD RISKS

How do top architects balance, navigate, and embrace the process of creating such large structures? What motivates their work? What do they aim for? David offers a unique perspective on these questions, especially when asked about what inspires him. Interestingly, his first response was about naysayers.

David's driving ambition is to make the world a better place. In college, he wrote on his résumé that his objective was to "improve the quality of the built environment through architectural design." A professor commented that this seemed overly ambitious for a new graduate, but David has kept this goal unchanged at the top of his résumé for forty years. "I never gave up on that concept, I never changed it, and it's still my main goal today," he said. This unwavering ambition has driven his career and guided his architectural endeavors.

His opening remark emphasized the need for self-belief in aspirations. Critics can chip away, but a strong foundation allows for risk-taking, which is vital for creativity. But how do we muster the courage for creative risks? Consider I. M. Pei's iconic Louvre pyramid, initially mocked for its contrast with the museum's traditional style. Now it stands as a celebrated symbol of architectural innovation. This example highlights the importance of coming up with a bold idea in the face of skepticism.

David identified two types of risk-taking in architecture: creative and practical. Creatively, he encourages taking risks and testing many ideas to see what works. "You need to be willing to throw a lot of ideas at the wall and see if any of them stick," he said. However, as an architect, he is cautious about risks that might alienate the public. "My design work tends to be a little bit on the conservative side because I like to respect history and context." This balance allows him to innovate while honoring the architectural legacy of cities.

David told us about the importance of openness to possibilities. During his consulting work with Fortune 50 companies in the '90s, he noticed that many managers were hesitant to suggest unconventional ideas because their careers had trained them to follow rules and meet expectations. As an outsider, David felt free to propose bold ideas without worrying about consequences, which often left the managers stunned. "The willingness to be open to new ideas is the essence of creativity," he said. This openness allowed him to bring a fresh perspective to brainstorming sessions, highlighting the value of thinking outside the box.

Almost all great leaders, creative mavericks, and superstars have faced setbacks and challenges in their careers. In his speech at the Basketball Hall of Fame, Michael Jordan noted how he used slights as motivation throughout his career. If India had been prosperous and democratic, Gandhi would never have emerged. Circumstance often pushes leaders into their roles. David shared his story of playing the long game and how it might all have never happened.

After thirty years of steady employment, David found himself jobless in 2010 at age fifty-three. With little hope of being hired during a recession, he decided to start his own firm, Convergence Design. The transition was accelerated when a consultant friend asked for help with a project. "It almost launched itself at that point, so I didn't have to do a whole lot of soul-searching," he explained. Over the next decade, Convergence Design grew step by step out of necessity, proving that sometimes adversity can lead to new and rewarding opportunities.

∦ CREATIVE SPARKS 1 ∦

Reflect on your own work and identify any bold, outlandish concepts you may have shied away from. Consider how embracing these ideas could lead to innovation and growth. Write down at least one bold idea you've had and plan a small, risk-free experiment to test its potential.

INTEGRATING CREATIVITY WITH LIFE BALANCE

The stereotypical image of creatives often depicts them as being on the edge, starving, or living in a constant state of mania. But is this really the case? Are there ways to integrate creativity into both work and home life more harmoniously? With advancements in technology and a more open approach to what constitutes a "normal" work schedule, we can redefine how we live and create. David seized this opportunity to reconfigure his life after unexpectedly losing the job he had held for thirty years.

"In the early aughts, I went through a transformation and realized my life was compartmentalized," David explained. "A lot of men have this problem, where you're one self at work, a different self at home, and another person in the community. I vowed that if I ever launched my own design firm, it would be called Convergence Design, to bring all those different selves together into an integrated person."

This philosophy of integration means being the same person at all times, and in the community. David shares this concept with potential employees to ensure it resonates with them. "I'm looking for somebody who really understands and values their commitments outside of work and wants to integrate them into a holistic life," he said. This approach fosters a sense of agency among his team, allowing them to organize their lives to balance personal and professional commitments effectively.

At his firm, David explained, flexibility and self-autonomy are key: "People organize their schedules around what's important to them, whether it's sleep, childcare, or other commitments. If Convergence Design were a large organization, this might not work, but at our size, it works very well." This flexibility empowers employees to manage their time and energy, leading to higher productivity and satisfaction.

⚡ CREATIVE SPARKS 2 ⚡

Reflect on how you're juggling work and life. Instead of striving for perfect balance, focus on maintaining emotional balance. Prioritize quality over quantity—when you're working, be fully engaged, and when you're with loved ones, be present.

THE POWER OF VISUALIZATION IN DESIGN

Athletes use visualization to see themselves succeeding, refining their technique, and boosting their confidence. As a creative person, do you visualize the finished project and think about the people who will enjoy it? Does that increase your motivation? What kinds of mental rehearsal or imagery help you picture a finished project in your mind's eye?

"Visualizing how people are going to use the building that we design is the essence of being an architect," David said. "I'm playing out scenarios in my head, like what's this going to be like for the dad taking his kid to the game? How will people with mobility impairments access our buildings? These scenarios shape the design process."

David's method involves both mental imagery and physical drawing. While athletes visualize their actions mentally, architects need to draw that vision on paper or a computer screen to kickstart a project and be productive. It's a very physical act rather than just a mental one. Writers might need to sit down and write nonsense for an hour to warm up; similarly, architects need to get their muscles warm and the pen moving on paper. Even if the first ten drawings end up crumpled on the floor, it's all part of the process.

David recalled long meetings where architects would discuss a project endlessly without drawing anything. This lack of action frustrated him. "As a creator, it's so important to just get something down on paper and respond to it," he said. "This is essential in getting the creative process going." He assumes that the first thing he draws might be terrible but believes it's a crucial step in uncovering a valuable idea.

In mindset training, sweating the details in your imagery is crucial. For example, a batter may visualize the fans in the stadium, tapping his cleats to shake off some red clay, noting the weight of the bat, and feeling the heat of the sun on his helmet. Similarly, David puts himself in the shoes of spectators to ensure his designs preserve every sensory element of the ballpark. This detailed visualization helps in creating a vivid and immersive experience for the end users.

"You want people to have a great time, and in the case of a ballpark, part of the secret sauce is designing an environment that creates a sense of excitement and anticipation the entire time fans are there," David explained. "The question becomes how you can hold on to that energy between the players and spectators, even when someone gets up to buy a hot dog.

"We've seen a lot of innovations in that regard, like an open concourse where the restrooms and concession stands are outward, and the inward view is open to the field. This way, even while standing in line for snacks, fans can take in the sounds and energy of the game. If the crowd roars, they can see what's happening. We spend a lot of time thinking and talking about how we're going to preserve that energy and help people sense, anticipate, and experience it even when they're not in their seats."

Visualization is not just about seeing; it's about creating a multisensory experience in your mind. When David envisions a ballpark, he thinks about how the sights, sounds, and smells will all contribute to a memorable experience for the visitors. This holistic approach ensures that every detail enhances the overall atmosphere and keeps the energy alive throughout the event.

⚡ **CREATIVE SPARKS 3** ⚡

Reflect on a current project and step into the shoes of the person who will be interacting with it. Visualize the entire experience, focusing on every detail that could enhance their engagement. Write down these sensory details and incorporate them into your design process.

NAVIGATING THE FINISH LINE

In creative pursuits, the concept of completion can be elusive. Writers often mention that a manuscript is never truly finished—you simply stop editing. Leonardo da Vinci echoed this sentiment about art, stating that art is never truly finished, only abandoned. How do you approach this aspect of creation? When do you decide to pause or conclude your process and consider something finished? David offered intriguing insights into answering these timeless questions.

"It's true that ballparks are never finished," David said. "Because if you look back on the last ten that have been opened, I can guarantee you that all of them have had some kind of renovation project in the last few years. And that includes the two that I'm most closely associated with. So they're never finished in that regard, but I will confess something to you: unlike Leonardo and many other artists, I am willing to say something is done."

David learned a valuable lesson in a college art class. His teacher taught that a great drawing is the first line you put on the page, representing the whole sketch, with details and embellishments added later. "His point was that anytime he walked by your drawing pad, you should be able to say, 'The drawing is done.' That doesn't mean it can't get better. It just means that it's done at any point," David explained. This perspective has shaped his approach to design. Rather than pursuing perfection, he is willing to declare a project complete at various stages and then refine it.

Some architects get a bad rap for constantly changing their minds, even after construction has begun. David, however, is comfortable living with things as they are. "We go through many stages in the design process, but I want to say that the design is done at some point," he said.

In certain cases, you don't get to decide where the finish line is. When you lose a client, a game, or a project, what does it take to move on to the next endeavor? Are there habits or perspectives that allow you to engage in something in the moment and then move on when it has passed? Artists and athletes alike talk about being in the moment, the flow, and being present.

David used a baseball analogy to explain this mindset in architecture. "The rule of thumb in our profession is that an architect will get one out of five projects that they go after," he said. "I have found that to be generally true, which means a .200 batting average in architecture is kind of par for the course. If you can bat better than .200, you're doing pretty well. This means you need to have that ballplayer's 'shake it off' mentality. If you're going to lose eight out of the ten projects that you go after, you've got to be willing to say, 'Tomorrow's another day and we'll get the next one.'"

✔ CREATIVE SPARKS 4 ✔

Reflect on your "batting" percentage in your creative endeavors. Accept that you won't hit a home run every time and recognize your capacity limits. Embrace the process, learn from each experience, and celebrate progress over perfection.

SEEKING GROWTH AND GUIDANCE

After designing two major league ballparks, David felt liberated knowing what the first line of his obituary would be. "Having a career pinnacle to look back on freed me to pursue whatever I wanted," he reflected.

This sense of accomplishment allowed him to move on and explore new opportunities without being tethered to the past.

"The origin story of Convergence Design is that a consultant friend called me up and said, 'I've got this client in Enid, Oklahoma, that doesn't know what to do with their little facility,'" David said. "And what we ended up doing was creating a kind of civic center that was transformative in their downtown. The total project budget, if you add everything together, might have been $30 million, which is a tenth of what a ballpark costs. Maybe earlier in my career, I wouldn't have thought of it as a great project, but since I had already done these two major league ballparks, I was able to put all my energy into this small-town transformation.

"Having those big rocks in place meant I didn't need to worry about it anymore. The way I would put it in sports language is to say, 'After I've won the World Series, I can go ahead and coach Little League, because why not?'"

A young artist doesn't have this luxury, but a mentor can help smooth out the road ahead, or at least give a heads-up on where there may be potholes or speed bumps. David's development was fast-tracked by working closely alongside experienced professionals during his first few years on the job.

"There are a whole lot of lessons to impart to a young architect, and I love when I get the chance to do that," David said. "I always like to share a story from early in my career when I worked in a very small office that had six people in Wichita, Kansas. And I've always said that passing the registration exam was much more a result of working in that firm than what I learned in school. Because in a small office, you learn by osmosis from being around people who are more experienced and know more than you do and can handle the everyday stresses and strains of being an architect. That is far more important than anything I learned in the academic setting."

David's first piece of advice to a young architect is to work in a small firm where you can learn from those who have been at it longer. "The other thing is to always think about the end user. Many architects pitch their careers toward fame and glory, but when you angle your career this way, you end up designing for magazine editors and awards juries."

"I really encourage young architects to pitch their careers toward the public and the people who will actually use, live in, work in, and walk by their buildings," he added. "If you do good work, those things will take care of themselves. But even if you don't end up being an award-winning architect, you can have the satisfaction of having improved the built environment through architectural design."

⁄ CREATIVE SPARKS 5 ⁄

Inspired by David's willingness to embrace all projects, reflect on whether you hold back from opportunities that seem too small or outside your familiar territory. Approach new endeavors with a "winning the World Series" attitude, seeing every experience as a chance to learn and grow.

FROM SALAD BARS TO MAJOR LEAGUE BALLPARKS

Over time, our definition of success may evolve. Do you need to be acknowledged by critics, peers, or an audience? Are awards and accolades necessary? Reflecting on your own definitions of success, consider Marie Kondo's mantra: "Does it spark joy?"

"Early in my career, I went from a six-person architectural shop to the corporate offices of Pizza Hut Incorporated, which was also located in Wichita, Kansas, at the time," David said. "While I was a corporate architect at Pizza Hut, I designed a salad bar to go in a particular decor that we were doing in some of our two thousand stores. It proved to be so popular that they started replicating it in virtually every location. This is going back to the 1980s."

David reflected on this achievement with pride. "To me, it was a significant career accomplishment, even though it was just a salad bar. It was a piece of design successful enough to be rolled out nationwide by a company that presumably had some idea of what they were doing. I used to walk into random Pizza Huts in the '90s and go, 'Oh, there's my salad bar,' and it was actually very gratifying."

Designing major league ballparks is obviously a real treat, but David suggested that success should be independent of the scale and perceived importance of the project. "If you can design a good salad bar or a good office building, then that's a highlight. Just bring your best game to whatever it is that you're doing, even if it's a salad bar," he said.

For a young architect or creator who feels they have put in maximum effort, dealing with criticism may not come easily. When we invest our whole heart and soul into an artistic creation, it is certainly hard not to take feedback or even an offhand comment personally.

David has seen this firsthand with architecture students: "They do these big projects and then they have these sessions at the end of the semester, where they bring in a bunch of working architects to critique the student work. Students often find these critiques to be traumatic, and the critics can be very harsh. These traumas are things that they carry with them through their entire careers."

He stressed the importance of separating oneself from one's work. "When I taught a class at a community college years ago, I would say to the students, 'I'm going to talk about your work, but I want you to separate that from yourself and understand that while I may say things about your projects, I'm not saying them about you. I might tell you that this could be done better, and that could be done better, but it doesn't mean you're a terrible person or a terrible future architect. It just means these are things that can be improved upon.' I would try to help the students pull apart their personal selves from the work that was on display."

Younger creatives are filled with ambition and grand scales, and rightly so. Looking back over a lifetime portfolio, what really stands out as being the most satisfying, the truest to your early aspirations? Will it always be the biggest project? The most money made? Or might it be something smaller? Time can bring perspective and also allow you to see some of the downstream effects that weren't apparent in the moment.

"Getting back to this question of perspective and career pinnacles, not long after finishing the two ballparks that I designed, my firm reassigned me to work on convention centers," David said. "One of the first projects that we got was a very small convention center for the community of Dubuque, Iowa. They had a lovely spot right on the Mississippi River, and as I said earlier, I thought that now I'd won the World Series, I could coach Little League."

David continued, "Okay, this is not a major metro area, but it's a project that means something to this city. So we poured ourselves into the design of this little convention center that sits proudly on the banks of the Mississippi River. Now, with the benefit of fifteen years of hindsight, it's been a really transformative project in that community. And the lesson that I take away from that is that, sure, designing major league ballparks is great fun. But if as an architect all I had ever done was a transformative project in the downtown of Dubuque, that would've been enough of a career pinnacle for me.

"Just the idea of designing a building that changed how a city saw itself is a remarkable thing. I think the framing aspect of having done the major league ballparks was really just to free me from my ambition. It allowed me to pour myself wholeheartedly into smaller projects that maybe a younger me might have dismissed as being insignificant."

∿ CREATIVE SPARKS 6 ∿

Does your definition of success rely on external validation like awards or recognition? Consider Marie Kondo's mantra: "Does it spark joy?" Identify the projects or experiences in your life that truly ignite your passion, regardless of scale.

THE 5 Cs IN DAVID GREUSEL'S JOURNEY

David Greusel's journey from an aspiring architect to a renowned designer of major league ballparks exemplifies the principles of mental toughness through the 5 Cs:

1. **Courage:** Launching Convergence Design during a recession marked a bold transition for David. His decision to open his own architectural practice amid financial uncertainty—starting with the revitalization of Enid, Oklahoma's civic center— showed remarkable bravery and had a transformative impact on communities.

2. **Confidence:** David's confidence drove him to pursue ambitious projects like PNC Park and Minute Maid Park. Ignoring early skepticism, he revolutionized ballpark design and maintained his vision of enhancing the built environment prominently on his résumé for four decades.

3. **Concentration:** David's meticulous approach to design focuses on quality and user experience. His innovative open concourse designs in ballparks evoke an engaging game atmosphere, a result of his deep concentration on enhancing fan experiences.

4. **Composure:** David consistently demonstrates composure under pressure. Whether designing massive ballparks or smaller projects like the convention center in Dubuque, Iowa, he methodically addresses challenges, ensuring each project's success through focused and steady leadership.

5. **Commitment:** David's commitment to enhancing the built environment is evident in every project. His approach, which marries creativity with historical and contextual respect, is encapsulated in his firm's name, Convergence Design, reflecting his dedication to creating spaces that resonate deeply within their communities.

YOUR CREATIVE TOOLKIT

Just as David Greusel exemplifies the 5 Cs of creativity through his remarkable career as a celebrated architect, you too can develop these strengths. Here are practical tips and tools based on the 5 Cs of creativity, inspired by his journey.

1. **Courage:**
   - **Empower with Visual Cues:** Enhance your creative workspace with visual reminders of courage, such as a motivating phone wallpaper or posters featuring powerful symbols like a lion. These constant visual cues will remind you of your inner strength and resilience while you work.
   - **Carry Tokens of Bravery:** Carry an object that embodies courage, like a stone from a tough hike or a piece of worn climbing rope. These tangible reminders of your strength can ground you and inspire you during challenging moments. For instance, you can keep it in your pocket or bag to touch whenever you need a boost of confidence.
   - **Visualize Your Victories:** When facing a creative hurdle, hold your courage object and visualize overcoming the obstacle. Imagine successfully navigating the challenge and achieving your goal. These visual and tactile cues, both in your workspace and on the go, help you stay focused on your goals and remind you of your strength to conquer any challenge.

2. **Confidence:**
   - **Cultivate Optimistic Confidence:** Excellence requires an abundance of both confidence and optimism. Let pessimism pass through your mind like a fleeting tunnel. For instance, if you think, "Something bad might happen, and I'll be overwhelmed and fail," acknowledge it and let it go. Then welcome optimistic thoughts like a refreshing breeze: "Something good might happen, and I'll learn and grow from the opportunity." Expecting positive outcomes keeps you focused on creation and wards off negativity.
   - **Identify and Celebrate Strengths:** Break down large tasks into smaller, manageable parts. Focus on areas where you excel to boost your confidence. Write down your strengths, such as creativity, resilience, and adaptability, and refer to them whenever self-doubt arises.
   - **Speak with Conviction:** Recognize that you are an expert

in your creative field. When speaking publicly about your craft, trust in your knowledge and experience. Your response doesn't need to be perfect; it just needs to reflect your expertise. If needed, ask for time to formulate your answer.

3. **Concentration:**
   - **Create a Focus-Driven Environment:** Forget clock-watching and worrying about what others are thinking or doing. Avoid visual disruptions and focus solely on your task. Peak performance is about the intensity and focus of your efforts, not the number of hours logged.
   - **Practice Silent Reflection:** Dedicate five to ten minutes daily to sit in silence, free from distractions. Close your eyes, focus on your breath, and let thoughts arise without judgment. Notice how quiet contemplation sparks new ideas and insights.
   - **Engage in Mindful Walking:** During a walk, shift your attention from your to-do list to the present moment. Focus on each step and the sensation of moving through space. Notice the feeling of your feet touching the ground and the rhythm of your pace. Allow your mind to relax and see what creative thoughts emerge naturally.

4. **Composure:**
   - **Transform Setbacks into Fuel:** When disappointment strikes, reframe it as a sign of your passion and dedication. Declare: "My creative fire burns bright, and I'll harness it to find solutions and new perspectives."
   - **Gradually Shift from Perfectionism to Progress:** Ditch the all-or-nothing mindset! Evaluate your work on a 1–100 scale, focusing on growth and incremental wins. Affirm: "I celebrate progress, not perfection, and find joy in the journey."
   - **Embrace the Beauty of Imperfection:** Give yourself permission to create "good enough" work sometimes. Remember, masterpieces are rare, and growth happens in the in-between. Repeat: "I welcome imperfection as a stepping-stone to creative evolution and learning."

5. **Commitment:**
    - **Craft with Love:** Passion fuels progress—loving your craft is the key to growth. Dive deep into your work, identify areas to refine, and challenge yourself to push boundaries. The more you embrace the process, the sharper your skills become. Stay committed to constant improvement, and watch your creativity evolve into greatness.
    - **Embrace the Messy Magic:** The messy middle can feel daunting, but it's where the magic happens! When things get tough, don't give up—push through. Struggles build strength, and each challenge is an opportunity to grow, learn, and create something extraordinary. So, keep moving forward, and remember: it's the hard parts that make the journey truly worthwhile.
    - **Earn Your Mentors by Offering Value:** Find mentors who fan your creative flames, but offer value first. Share their work, leave positive reviews, or support them in ways that matter. By giving before you take, you create a stronger, reciprocal relationship. These mentors will push you to grow, believing in your talent while offering guidance. Approach mentorship with respect and reciprocity.

IN THE NEXT CHAPTER

Precision meets passion in Graham Thompson's expert hands, transforming hatmaking into an art form. Known for meticulous attention to detail and a relentless pursuit of excellence, Graham has redefined bespoke craftsmanship. Discover the secrets behind his mastery and the insights that inspire.

Chapter 8

THE HATTER'S BENCH: GRAHAM THOMPSON

*W*earing *a vintage blue denim shirt, oilcloth apron, and one of his own handcrafted hats perched on his head, the hatmaker leans over the wooden workbench. The reds, yellows, and oranges of its grain contrast with the black fedora resting on it. He picks up the hat, places it on a vintage machine—its aged steel nearly a century old—and steam rises as if from an old train funnel. The heat and moisture soften the felt, and he shapes the brim so the wearer can set it at a rakish angle. Each movement is a testament to his mastery and devotion to the craft. It takes two months to finish a single fedora in this classic way, and three times that for a straw Montecristi to fully form. Only this patient combination of care, traditional methods, and expert craftsmanship can produce an Optimo Hat.*

Back in the '80s, it was rare for a teenager to venture across South Chicago to hang out in a hat shop. But on Saturday mornings, Graham's parents knew they'd find their son watching master hatmaker Johnny Tyus practice his art and chat with loyal customers. At sixteen, Graham decided to buck the fashion trends of his peers and establish a distinctive style harkening back to the Golden Age of Hollywood and the Jazz

Age. When he asked in a local department store where to find headwear like Robert Mitchum, James Cagney, or Humphrey Bogart wore, the sales manager sent him to Johnny's Hat Shop on 79th and Racine.

"Johnny told me, 'I suggest you buy an old hat from the '30s or '40s, and I'll clean it up for you,'" Graham said. "So I placed ads in the newspapers and eventually found black and blue fedoras. I took them to Johnny, and he restored them. By the time I was eighteen, I'd saved up $250, enough for him to make me my first custom hat."

FORGING A PATH OF PASSION

In his journey toward mastery, Graham's fascination with vintage hats began early, not just with their aesthetics but in mastering the intricate techniques of cleaning, restoration, and construction. His commitment to excellence set him apart, ensuring each hat was not just an accessory, but a piece of art.

He dedicated himself to unraveling the secrets behind their durability and superior quality, spending countless hours learning from Johnny's expert craftsmanship. This hands-on experience behind the counter was transformative, offering Graham firsthand insights into the meticulous artistry that distinguishes premium hats from mass-produced ones. The attention to detail and the love infused into each hat became Graham's signature.

While his peers chased fleeting fashion trends, Graham remained steadfast in his admiration for classic hats. His choice reflected not only a preference in style but also a profound respect for disappearing artisanal skills, amid a culture increasingly dominated by mass-market influences. This unique blend of curiosity and individuality marked Graham early on, shaping a path that intertwined passion with purpose.

After wrapping up his senior year, Graham decided to study international trade and finance at Chaminade University in Honolulu, where the tropical humidity and pristine beaches were a far cry from the harsh Midwest winters he had grown up with. A semester in Kyoto further enriched his journey, exposing him to the deep dedication and creativity of local artisans—a reflection of the same spirit that had captivated him in Johnny's Hat Shop.

Reflecting on his time in Japan, Graham remarked, "I encountered contrasting lifestyles—the regimented 'company man' culture alongside the artistry and simplicity of small businesses and traditional crafts. It was a moment of realization—I yearned for a life immersed in creativity, craftsmanship, and meaningful pursuits rather than conforming to corporate norms."

⚡ CREATIVE SPARKS 1 ⚡

Consider a passion project you love deeply, regardless of external validation. What ignites your curiosity and desire to learn and grow? Identify one specific way you can integrate this passion into your daily life starting today.

THE PURSUIT OF HATMAKING EXCELLENCE

After returning to Chicago post-graduation, Graham faced an unexpected twist: Johnny Tyus announced his retirement and the imminent closure of his hat shop. Rather than signaling an end, this unforeseen development opened a new chapter in Graham's quest for hatmaking excellence. Faced with the possibility of his mentor's legacy fading away, Graham felt a profound responsibility to preserve and elevate the art form.

"In the back of my mind, I always harbored a desire to learn a rare craft and create something with my own hands," Graham said. "As a child, I was fascinated by watchmaking, dreamed of moving to Switzerland for it, and was inspired by vintage cars and fine woodworking. Part of this stemmed from my curiosity about what principles lead to excellence in any field. Plus, I had this entrepreneurial dream of owning a shop. Johnny's Hat Shop presented a unique opportunity to blend both aspirations—acquiring a craft and running my own store."

The road ahead was strewn with challenges that tested Graham's resolve and financial limits. "The first year was unbelievably tough," Graham recalled. "I assumed the purchase price for the shop covered training with Johnny, but it only included equipment and his clientele. We had to negotiate a separate fee for his mentorship, based on a percentage of our earnings.

"It's remarkable how much thirstier you are for knowledge when you're paying for everything. We'd work together all day, I'd go back to the apartment above the shop, and then we'd start again the next day. I thought the word would soon spread about the business and the money would start coming in, but instead I had to max out multiple credit cards. I took hats from dry cleaners and even cleaned baseball caps to make a little extra money. I worked really hard, risked a lot, and barely made it."

Even as his determination fueled his growth as both a craftsman and a business owner, the early days were fraught with uncertainty and self-doubt. "Three months into owning the shop, fear crept in," Graham said. "I stood outside one night, peering in. The shop was new and pristine but lacked the ambiance I envisioned. Business was slow, finances were tight, and doubts flooded my mind. I broke down, fearing failure. But the next morning, I chose a different mental stance. I reminded myself of those facing tougher challenges and reframed my outlook. It was a pivotal moment." From that point on, Graham's positive mindset and commitment to quality served as guiding beacons.

Unsatisfied with mere mastery, Graham embarked on a global quest for elements that would help him create the finest hats. "For twenty-five years, I've been on a treasure hunt for the finest materials and tools," Graham shared. "Sometimes I'll discover something in a museum that will improve the quality of a hat. We've also made custom machines that improve some aspects of our operation and created a custom hatter's bench. When you put those little details together, it makes your products more sublime and special.

"I want to put so much love and craft into each piece that it becomes an heirloom," Graham said. "I like doing things properly—you can feel and see the difference in quality that it makes. How could you not do your very best? It's ingrained in me."

⚡ CREATIVE SPARKS 2 ⚡

Reflect on a skill or knowledge you desire that demands dedication and perseverance. What steps can you take to start your own "treasure hunt" for learning and growth? Remember, the journey can be as rewarding as the destination.

FINE-TUNING THE PERFECT WORKSPACE

Peering behind the veil of Graham's meticulous hatmaking process reveals a world of intricacy and passion. While business development and customer interactions at Optimo's shop in the Monadnock Building on West Jackson occupy his time, Graham finds true bliss back at the hatter's bench where Optimo Hats first took shape, now nestled within a 7,700-square-foot former firehouse transformed by his vision in 2015.

The space itself mirrors the artistry of an Optimo hat, thanks to the striking design by Chicago architecture firm Skidmore, Owings & Merrill (SOM). By accentuating the building's classic elements, like the original brick and the void where the fireman's pole once stood, and blending this with innovative additions, such as the cozy lounge adorned with over a thousand of Graham's vinyl records, the design fosters an environment conducive to his finest work.

"There's a sense of happiness I only get from hatmaking," Graham shared. "It feels great to be in that flow state. Once I get into a rhythm, I'm not thinking about anything else. When I turn my phone and everything else off, I have a hundred percent focus. Essentialism leads to me having more of these flow state moments. We've all got limited time. So what do you want to do with it? What do you want to be great at?"

While venturing into new territories and addressing weaknesses is crucial for any creator, Graham remains steadfast in prioritizing the passion that initially led him to apprentice under Johnny Tyus: crafting the world's finest hats.

"I try to live by the Marcus Aurelius quote 'Do less, better,'" Graham said. "In my business, it's about focusing on doing one thing very well. We are going to stay in our lane, respect our materials, and double down on hatmaking." Graham's commitment to this Stoic philosophy translates into cutting back on material possessions and eliminating subtractive rituals. This minimalist approach allows him to focus deeply on whatever he's doing.

"Society says you need all this stuff, but there are many things and routines that don't bring happiness. They're nonessentials. I try to carefully curate my life, workdays, and social circles, prioritizing what I love doing and what touches my heart. There's so much joy in simplicity."

As Optimo's business expands, Graham's involvement in various aspects grows. However, to deliver his best work, he understands the necessity of uninterrupted concentration. In their new workshop, designed specifically for hatmaking, efficiency and precision are paramount. Every corner of the workshop is a testament to Graham's commitment to quality and craftsmanship.

In his book *Turning Pro: Tap Your Inner Power and Create Your Life's Work*, Steven Pressfield underscores the importance of a dedicated workspace. For a hatter, this means a bench with ample space for tools, a strategic workflow, and proximity to machines. In Optimo's new facility, every space is purpose-built, allowing them to merge precision and efficiency seamlessly.

Graham's obsession with research and development manifests in Optimo's machinery, tools, and materials meticulously arranged to ensure consistency and support his relentless pursuit of hatmaking perfection.

"I've set up this workshop for the highest-quality work. A clean workspace without clutter aids in organization and precision. I don't want to have to stop and look for a certain tool or mold—that messes with my mind. I just need to concentrate on the hat I'm working on. With more space and custom-built tools, we achieve hyper-accuracy in fit and finish. When we elevate quality, there's no downside—our hats feel better, look better, fit better, and age better."

⚡ CREATIVE SPARKS 3 ⚡

Visualize your perfect workspace. Is it distraction-free, enabling you to achieve a "flow state"? What tools and resources are essential for your excellence? How can you establish a dedicated space or routine to enhance your process?

BALANCING ART AND BUSINESS

While mastering the art of hatmaking, Graham also faced the challenge of juggling creativity and commerce. Growing up in Chicago, he observed his father transition from working at General Motors for two decades to building custom homes with some of the city's most respected architects.

Despite being a good businessman, Graham's father was an artist at heart, always adding extra details to enhance homeowners' experiences. These artistic touches often increased costs and reduced profit margins—a tradeoff many master artisans make in pursuit of excellence.

"When artistry is inside of you and that's your greatest passion, you follow that path," Graham said. "But this often doesn't lead to the most money. I have this affliction—I'm an entrepreneur and a craftsman. I would be more financially successful if my passion for making money matched my creative drive, but it doesn't. As soon as I have a few bucks, I invest in the next improvement. Yet I believe if I just make a hat far and away the best, success will follow."

Achieving such success requires Graham and his team to practice an extraordinary level of patience. In a world that demands instant gratification, creating a fine hat that lasts decades is a painstaking process. Graham limits Optimo's production to 2,500–3,000 hats a year, maintaining rigorous quality control, contrary to the Silicon Valley creed of rapid growth.

"With some of the finest straw materials, it can take months to make a single piece," he said. "There used to be more pride in true craftsman-ship, rejecting inferior pieces. We're careful about partnerships because few can meet the standards required to weave such straws. We honor that skill in finishing every hat. You need more diligent selection, better processes, and a determination never to send out work below your usual high standards."

Though a creator first and entrepreneur second, Graham has had to become proficient in sales, management, financials, and other areas cru-cial for a small business. "When I started, I was very green and didn't real-ize all the expenses involved. Selling a hat for a thousand dollars didn't mean that was all profit. You need awareness of what it takes to succeed if pursuing your passion full time. Talk to industry people, understand the challenges, and write a business plan, even if just for yourself."

Graham's original plan didn't include creating for film and television, but as he became one of the most well-respected hatmakers in the world, the entertainment industry took notice. If you've seen memorable Holly-wood hats on screen recently, they were probably crafted by Graham and his small team. From the hats for Woody Harrelson and Kevin Costner in *The Highwaymen* to Russell Crowe in *Cinderella Man* to Johnny Depp's John Dillinger in *Public Enemies*, costume designers frequently return to Optimo.

Graham collaborates closely with three-time Academy Award winner Colleen Atwood to ensure that hats in her films perfectly complement the costumes and sets. This active role allows Graham to influence the kind of films that inspired him to start wearing hats.

"The best hats are a combination of design and quality. You don't have to be a connoisseur to see the difference, whether in person or on the big screen. It's great to see directors re-creating films with hats and wanting the best they can find."

Such quality has also made Graham the go-to hatter for musicians like Eddie Vedder and Jack White, golfer Tiger Woods, and actor Andy Garcia. Thanks to style setter John Lee Hooker, Optimo has become a favorite among many bluesmen. Graham remains connected to the rich hat and clothing culture in South Chicago, drawing inspiration from the stylish regulars he first saw at Johnny's Hat Shop. "These were some of the coolest cats I'd ever seen," Graham recalled. "The way they'd walk and talk, each with a unique way of wearing their hats."

Despite growing his business to the point of expanding from the original building on 102nd and Western, attracting Hollywood collaborators, and making Optimo Hats the de facto choice for celebrities and discerning collectors alike, Graham's resolve and revenue were shaken by the COVID-19 pandemic. As small and midsize companies of all stripes struggled, and many went out of business, he had to dig deep to keep the lights on and steady his mental state with a healthy dose of perseverance.

"When the pandemic first hit, we were in a strong position, but within a few months, I was struggling to pay our mortgages," Graham recalled. "There were several times when I panicked and thought we might have to close for good. But then I thought of the people we source our materials from, the customers I serve, and how much I love what I do, and that kept me going."

⚡ CREATIVE SPARKS 4 ⚡

Reflect on how you balance creative passion with business needs, as Graham did. Identify one actionable step to excel in your field while ensuring financial sustainability. Schedule a monthly "Business of Creativity" review to track progress, adjust strategies, and focus on mastering the entrepreneurial side of your craft.

FINDING STRENGTH IN CREATIVE COMMUNITY

Whether crafting hats for an A-list celebrity or a local regular, Optimo ensures that every detail—from the camber of the brim to the feather tucked into the luxe ribbon to the care instructions on the inside of the hat box—is meticulously attended to. This requires close collaboration with the suppliers and partners Graham carefully chooses to be part of his community.

"A craftsman is somebody who is always striving to improve," Graham said. "The deeper your understanding of every facet of what you're creating, the better. The closer I get to the makers of our components and raw materials, the greater the impact on the hats we make. For our straws, for instance, I've always brought examples of the finest hats ever made to show weavers and merchants the kind of consistency I'm looking for. And the same thing goes for our felts. It starts with researching the history behind what you're trying to do and then advancing those practices as far as you can."

The image often associated with Optimo features Graham alone at his hatter's bench, so it's easy to imagine him toiling solo as he puts the techniques Johnny Tyus taught him into practice. Yet, while the life of an artist is often solitary, Graham has found support in cultivating a small community of like-minded creators that includes chefs, luxury carmakers, and winemakers.

"Even though someone might be in an entirely different industry, there's a camaraderie between us," Graham said. "They might be running a much larger business with more clients, but many of the challenges, problems, and frustrations are the same. We also find that we're pursuing common principles and finding similar joys in doing the best possible work we can."

Graham finds great pleasure in discussing craftsmanship with fellow artisans. These conversations often spark new ideas and innovative approaches to their respective disciplines. "It's so much fun talking about how we approach our crafts, and a commitment to making the best possible products is a common thread. We also discuss how to take our companies to the next level from a business perspective. There's some scale that is ideal for lifestyle, artistry, quality, and taking care of your customers," he explained.

Gratitude is one of the most underrated mental skills for any creator. Being thankful for your art, the people who support you, and the opportunity to share it with the world helps you push through difficult days. For Graham, his gratitude blends with an appreciation of continuing

Johnny Tyus's legacy in Chicago and beyond. He feels proud to have carried the torch onward, meeting incredible people and embarking on journeys worldwide.

"It's about approaching both the business and the art as a craft," Graham said. "It's a spiritual path in a way. It's fun, enjoyable, and fits my skills."

Graham's love for what he does and his desire to elevate hatmaking drive him forward. "I was passed a torch, and I'm proud that I took it onward. I love what I do. I'm grateful to have met the most incredible people and for the journeys that have taken me to countries all over the world." This sense of gratitude has been a cornerstone in his perseverance and success.

It's easy for a creator to have ambitions and goals but never pursue them, often making excuses or settling for a supposedly safe career. Graham could have made a lot of money in international finance. Instead, he took over an old man's hat shop, learned a seemingly dying trade, and advanced it. "While you could bring romance to any profession, I can't imagine working in a job that I didn't like or doing anything mediocre," Graham remarked.

Reflecting on his journey, Graham emphasized the importance of unwavering dedication and enthusiasm. "If you know your dream, follow it through, and know what good looks like, you'll probably make it. But you've got to be really into it, so you don't lose your initial excitement. You need to be obsessed. If you are, you love it, and you have talent, then go for it."

⚡ CREATIVE SPARKS 5 ⚡

Reflect on Graham's dedication and resilience. Is there a dream you've set aside? Small steps, like seeking mentors or joining a supportive community, can fuel your journey. What's one action you can take today to pursue your passion?

THE 5 Cs IN GRAHAM THOMPSON'S JOURNEY

Graham Thompson's journey from a passionate teenager fascinated by vintage hats to a master hatmaker and successful entrepreneur exemplifies the principles of mental toughness through the 5 Cs:

1. **Courage:** Graham demonstrated remarkable courage when he took over Johnny's Hat Shop, faced financial uncertainties, and overcame a steep learning curve with bravery. After Johnny's retirement announcement, Graham embraced the challenge of mastering a rare craft and running a business, showcasing his readiness to tackle the unknown.

2. **Confidence:** Graham's confidence grew as he invested in high-quality materials and equipment, committed to achieving excellence in craftsmanship. His efforts to source the finest straw and collaborate with master weavers, even in remote regions, underscore his strong belief in his vision and his craft.

3. **Concentration:** Graham's meticulous attention to detail in hatmaking—from the curve of the brim to the finish—demonstrates his exceptional concentration. His ability to enter a flow state while working ensures that each hat meets his high standards of quality.

4. **Composure:** During the pandemic, Graham maintained his composure despite financial strains, driven by his passion for the craft and commitment to his customers. His calm approach and innovative strategies helped his business survive and thrive in tough times.

5. **Commitment:** Graham's commitment to quality and the legacy of hatmaking shines through his use of the finest materials and traditional techniques. His meticulous approach and continual refinement of his craft underscore his dedication to creating the world's finest hats.

YOUR CREATIVE TOOLKIT

Just as Graham Thompson exemplifies the 5 Cs of mental toughness in his journey as the owner of Optimo, elevating hatmaking to an art form, you too can develop these strengths. Here are practical tips and tools based on the 5 Cs of creativity, inspired by his journey.

1. **Courage:**
   - **Face Fear Head-On:** Identify what type of fear is holding you back. Is it fear of failure, of rejection, or of not being good enough? Acknowledge the specific fear and its source to better understand and manage it.
   - **See Through the Fear:** Close your eyes, breathe deeply, and picture yourself walking through a dense, dark cloud symbolizing fear. As you move forward, imagine the cloud dissipating, revealing a bright, clear path ahead. Visualize yourself emerging with confidence and determination.
   - **Declare Your Bravery:** Proclaim, "I am courageous. Every challenge strengthens my creative spirit." Embrace the bravery needed to pursue your creative dreams, and let this affirmation empower you to face any obstacle with strength.

2. **Confidence:**
   - **Affirm Your Creative Power:** Begin each day with powerful affirmations, like "I am a creative powerhouse." Work the mirror when you repeat it—look yourself in the eyes and assertively reinforce this belief in your mind. Say with confidence, "My ideas flow freely," to set a positive tone for your day and empower your creative process.
   - **Fully Own Your Past Successes:** Embrace your past achievements and let them fuel your confidence. Don't diminish them with thoughts like "It was just a school project" or "I only played a small part." You earned those

wins, and they're proof you have what it takes. Celebrate them, and let that success propel you toward new challenges.

- **Quickly Replace Doubt with Belief:** When self-doubt creeps in, replace it with empowering thoughts. Ask yourself, "Is this thought helping me grow?" If not, swap it for a confident affirmation. You control your mindset—believe in yourself and unlock your full creative potential.

3. **Concentration:**
   - **"WIN" the Moment:** When distracted, regain focus with a simple question: "What's Important Now?" to refocus on the present task and prioritize your goals.
   - **"NBA" Your Mistakes:** Embrace the NBA approach: "Next Best Action." When errors occur, shift your energy from dwelling on mistakes to taking productive action. Ask yourself, "What's the next best thing I can do right now?"
   - **WIN with NBA Mindset:** Combine the power of both acronyms by asking yourself "What's Important Now?" and following up with "Next Best Action." This one-two punch helps you stay focused, overcome obstacles, and maintain a productive mindset.

4. **Composure:**
   - **Control Your Narrative:** Let go of what's outside your control and view external circumstances as neutral. When faced with unexpected challenges, label them as "just what is" and focus on what you can control: your response, creative process, and interpretation.
   - **Amplify Positivity:** Shift your focus to the good by contrasting it with the bad. Top performers emphasize positive experiences, using them to boost confidence and joy. View negative experiences objectively, without emotional attachment, to learn and grow.
   - **Balance Drive and Joy:** Harmonize ambition with appreciation to transform your creative journey. Ambition fuels improvement and growth, while appreciation

keeps you grounded and joyful. Celebrate progress, savor moments, and maintain a sustainable drive to enhance resilience.

5. **Commitment:**
   - **Align Passion with Purpose:** Fuel your creativity by setting goals that merge your passion with a purpose you care deeply about. If you love storytelling, for example, create a children's book that teaches resilience. If music is your passion, compose songs that inspire hope. Aligning passion with purpose adds depth and meaning to your work, making it resonate more powerfully with your audience.
   - **Pursue Growth Opportunities:** Challenge yourself with new experiences that inspire growth. Take workshops, explore new mediums, try new art supplies, travel, or collaborate with others. These experiences refresh your creativity and spark new ideas and techniques to explore.
   - **Translate Knowledge into Action:** Bridge the gap between intention and action. Identify the skills you want to master, schedule time for focused practice, and track your progress. Celebrate your wins to build momentum and stay motivated. Turn your knowledge into results and watch your creative goals come to life.

IN THE NEXT CHAPTER

Where artistry meets fearless expression, step into the world of Dom Streater, a *Project Runway* champion whose bold designs and innovative vision have redefined modern fashion. Discover how her creative journey inspires aspiring designers to break boundaries and embrace their individuality.

Chapter 9

MAKING EACH STITCH COUNT: DOM STREATER

A young girl watches intently as her mother carefully lets down the hem of her dress. Unable to afford a new Catholic school uniform each semester, her mother relies on creativity and resourcefulness. Every stitch sows a seed in her daughter's mind, not only extending the garment's life but also creating a world of possibilities for her future. One day, this little girl will create from a place of passion rather than necessity, with the world watching.

Fast-forward a few years, when Dom Streater has found herself in her mother's place. Though not in front of the classic old sewing machine yet, she received an entry-level one as a Christmas gift, picked from the crisp pages of the JCPenney catalog that arrived in the mailbox like clockwork each December. "She taught me how to sew buttons back on my blouses and take up or let down my skirt hems," Dom recalled. "Growing up, sewing was just a utility because our family didn't have much money. I knew well enough not to ask my mom for anything, as I knew how hard she worked for us in radiology in the ER. She was in the trenches."

Her mom's demanding work schedule left Dom and her brother with a lot of free time at their grandmother's house. While some of their peers in West Philadelphia might have used this time to get into trouble, Dom's brother played on his Nintendo and watched music videos, and Dom began exploring various kinds of art. She wasn't the only creative kid in the neighborhood. "One time I overheard my art teacher saying, 'Willie is such a sweet boy,' to a colleague and later realized she was talking about Will Smith," Dom said. "His company is called Overbrook Entertainment because we're from the same part of Philly."

DOM'S ARTISTIC BEGINNING

While Will Smith channeled his talent into rapping and acting in *The Fresh Prince of Bel-Air*—where his character was "West Philadelphia, born and raised"—Dom preferred painting and fashion design from a young age.

"I sketched designs and made clothes for my Barbies out of construction paper," Dom said. Her early creative endeavors were driven purely by personal joy, without the pressure of external judgment. "As an artist, you can get too wrapped up in what others might think and stifle your decision-making because of that. But as a kid, I was creating just for me. I love the notion of doing something for its own sake. For writers, artists, designers, and musicians, there's something about going back to that innocence of being creative and not worrying so much. I think that we get stuck in our heads."

Dom's passion for fashion led her to Moore College in her hometown for further education. Despite being self-taught and having always learned by doing, she recognized the value of structured learning to refine her craft.

"I didn't know the Fibonacci method or the rule of thirds—I was a blank canvas and had no SOP [standard operating procedure] because I didn't come from a creative family," she explained. "Moore College helped me set up some guardrails and understand how the fashion industry works."

During her time at Moore, Dom seized opportunities to gain practical experience through internships. A significant one involved setting up fashion shoots for *Complex* magazine.

"Completing a fashion merchandising and styling internship for a fashion magazine led to me looking at garments with a 360-degree view, whereas a lot of designers tend to just think about the front visual of it," Dom explained. "I tend to think about the woman coming and going too. Because *Complex* is a men's magazine and I was surrounded by guys, I had to start considering clothing in a new way and could take myself out of the equation."

⚡ CREATIVE SPARKS 1 ⚡

Great creations are rarely solo endeavors. Reflect on the artists, mentors, or friends who have championed your journey. How has their support become a vital piece of your creative puzzle?

GETTING RUNWAY READY

When Dom began gaining real-world experience through internships, she discovered that blazing her own trail in fashion and textile design wasn't just acceptable—it was preferable.

"Working at *Complex* showed me that there are rules when it comes to designing clothing," Dom said. "You don't have to always follow them, but you need to know what they are to play the game. Once I knew that, it flipped a switch because then I had permission to throw the rule book out the window. That's when I really started to have fun, instead of trying to follow what someone told me was the standard. I'd think, 'No, that's the baseline.' Where you go with it is up to you."

Dom's internship at *Complex* also strengthened her work ethic. "We'd have to arrive for shoots early each morning, and I often wouldn't get home again until after midnight," she said. Later, she worked for Peter Som, who was the creative director for Bill Blass and a consultant for Tommy Hilfiger, designing the women's wear collection. "I learned a lot about patternmaking and different ways to approach the technical side of textiles," Dom said.

It would be logical to assume that Dom went straight into the fashion business after graduating from Moore College. Instead, she took a diversion and returned to something she had loved as a teenager. "I was in animal care during four years of high school," Dom said. "I worked with orangutans, gorillas, lemurs, monkeys, reptiles, highland cattle, and rabbits at the Philadelphia Zoo—I ran the gamut. After college the economy was terrible, and not a lot of fashion brands were hiring. So I went back into animal care at the University of Pennsylvania for three years. I was also a restaurant hostess and server, and I did some bartending. My mom let me live with her for a long time."

While she loved the peace that tending to animals gave her (and the fact that they didn't talk back), holding down three jobs started to wear on Dom and impede her creativity. "I was getting burned out, and on my off days I didn't have much energy left to create," she said. "I'd drape fabric on a dress form while I was listening to music or watching a movie, making sure I was making something. But I wasn't even sketching out these ideas."

Around the time she applied for *Project Runway*, Dom decided that she needed to share her designs with an audience. Some creators are paralyzed by their fear of criticism and rejection, but Dom craved some kind of reaction to her creations. She started looking for local fashion shows and found a multidisciplinary event called RAW Artists, which she entered and won.

Meanwhile, Dom's boyfriend saw how much she enjoyed watching the hit Lifetime show *Project Runway* and knew that she still loved making her own clothes. So he started encouraging her to try for a spot on the next season. "He kept saying, 'You should apply for this,' and I'd always tell him no," Dom said. "One day, I thought, 'Screw it,' and applied just to silence my inner monologue."

Dom was pleasantly surprised to get a callback from the show, but things didn't go according to plan. "Most people don't know that I wasn't selected for *Project Runway* season eleven," she said. "The producer told me, 'Do more and come back in a year.' That was a big deal, and I got discouraged because I was finally creating again and had done all this hard work, and it didn't matter.

"My parents are both incredibly hard workers, and my mom's expectation is always, 'You do the job, you don't half-ass it.' That helped me. And I got back into the research I'd started in high school. I'd saved stacks of sketchbooks from the art supply store, in which I put cutouts from fashion magazines like *Harper's*, *Vogue*, and *Nylon* that I'd get out of neighbors' recycling bins. I looked through all of those and started reading blogs and Reddit threads. I spent a lot of time absorbing all this print and digital stuff, and then I'd go sketch and drape. It was about gathering ideas, like the first time you visit other cultures abroad."

✁ CREATIVE SPARKS 2 ✁

Identify your creative foundations: the techniques, styles, or genres that define your work. Reflect on how they shape your creations. Then challenge one or two in your next project—like a painter breaking into digital art. This bold step will ignite innovation and elevate your creativity.

INTO THE WORKROOM

One day, Dom received a call that would change everything. It was from the same *Project Runway* producer who, twelve months earlier, had decided Dom wasn't ready. He invited her to New York for a closed audition. Excited, Dom packed up five of her designs and called a friend to model them. They boarded a train from Philly and headed to meet the producer, perennial mentor Tim Gunn (who went on to present *Making the Cut* with supermodel and former *Project Runway* host Heidi Klum), and past winner Michael Costello.

"I felt much more confident and sure of myself because of all the research, sketching, and draping I'd done during that year," Dom said. "There weren't any of the weird moments that I'd had in the previous audition, and it felt right. They knew who I'd been before and who I'd become since."

Instead of waiting anxiously by her phone afterward, Dom went on a camping trip. While she was away, she got a call from a New York area code. Sure enough, it was the producer again, and she was cast in *Project Runway* season twelve.

What followed was a whirlwind. Dom packed a few supplies for the famous workroom at the Parsons School of Design in Greenwich Village and a couple of bags for the dorm-style housing that Lifetime provided contestants.

If the showrunners expected drama from Dom, they were soon disappointed by her poise and thoughtful demeanor. "I'm a very quiet person," she said. "I'm usually the friend at the table who says nothing until I have something to say, and that was my personality on *Project Runway*. I treated it like I was going to do a job: this is what I have to do. I'd rewatched every season and realized that there's a formula. I knew there would be makeover and teen challenges, and one using recycled materials. So I mentally prepared myself and had a blueprint in mind going in so that when I got there, I didn't feel overwhelmed."

Despite her game plan, Dom wasn't completely insulated from the ups and downs of her fellow designers. Some became friends, while others seemed intent on creating drama for its own sake.

Dom recounted an incident from her first day in the workroom. "One girl had never used a commercial sewing machine before," she said. "We were using parachute material, and she asked me to help wind her bobbin. I showed her how to do it, and you would've thought World War II had broken out by the way some of the other designers reacted."

They were shocked by her willingness to help. "Are you crazy?" and "Why would you help her? That's stupid—she's your competition!" were a few of the comments swirling around the room.

Dom found the backlash absurd. "One, she didn't know how to thread a sewing machine, and two, it took me about forty seconds of the eleven hours we were there that day," she explained. "That's when I decided I'd start observing instead of interacting, so I never got into an argument on the show."

↗ CREATIVE SPARKS 3 ↗

Define your ultimate creative goal. Just as Dom prepared for *Project Runway* by envisioning challenges and planning her approach, craft a focused statement that outlines your vision, key steps, and anticipated obstacles. This clarity will keep you focused, motivated, and confident throughout your journey.

THE ART OF STAYING COMPOSED

One of the most challenging aspects of *Project Runway* is the intense time constraints. Contestants are usually given only limited time to create a piece and just twelve weeks to design an entire collection for New York Fashion Week, if they advance that far. These extremely compressed timelines create a pressure cooker environment in the workroom.

Dom's mental fortitude was crucial to her success on the show. She focused on staying calm amid the chaos. "There was some weird behavior while the cameras were rolling, but I didn't feel the need to participate in that," Dom remarked. By choosing to observe rather than engage, she could concentrate on sketching her designs and selecting fabrics to bring her vision to life.

However, the *Project Runway* experience was not without its demands. "While the editing makes it look like we had less time than we did, it was still a one-day turnaround with very long hours," Dom explained. Contestants would start at 4:00 AM and work until around 11:00 PM, then get up before dawn to prepare for the day.

Dom described the exhaustion and how she had to force herself to eat breakfast for energy even when she wasn't hungry. The contestants often had to work with unconventional materials and one day were even blindfolded while they were driven to the location of a mystery challenge. In those chaotic moments, Dom wasn't sure how she'd respond or if she'd lose her creativity. Having a prepared mindset and a playbook as a backup plan was crucial.

Another key to Dom's composure was her Catholic faith. "There's something very soothing about having a moment of prayer for myself. It's like meditation, requiring you to quiet your mind and be still," she said. Those quiet moments helped her stay calm during the judges' critique in front of peers and a TV audience of millions.

Dom saw this as an opportunity to learn from seasoned designers like Michael Kors and fashion editor Nina Garcia. Although the critiques seemed brief on TV, they actually lasted around forty minutes to an hour. "They were honest discussions, but standing under hot stage lamps and talking back and forth with the judges was intense," Dom recalled. She found the critiques insightful, and especially valued Garcia's consistent and knowledgeable feedback. "You need to listen to advice but not let it impact you so much that your entire aesthetic changes."

After showcasing their work and hearing critiques, contestants faced a tense interlude before learning their fate. In the green room, they were not allowed to speak to each other to ensure everything was captured on camera. "You're left alone with your thoughts, questioning what you did and why you were safe," Dom said. She used this time for mental reflection, considering what she had made for the challenge.

Despite Dom's drama-free approach and calm demeanor on *Project Runway*, she had a fierce competitive spirit. "Being just 'safe' after a challenge was unacceptable to me," Dom said. This meant her design was merely adequate to progress to the next round, which felt like a lack of progress. "If I was bad, I'd get feedback to improve, and if I was good, I'd know I was on the right path," she explained.

Despite her frustration with limited feedback, Dom's unique designs set her apart. The judges often urged competitors to have a strong point of view, but Dom's distinctive patterns made her stand out from the start.

Being a textile designer, she wasn't content with the selection at Mood Fabrics (the store where contestants were brought to shop for materials), so she'd create her own. "I'd put all this energy and work into making these fabrics and designing this whole thing, only to hear, 'You're safe.' There was a part of me that was like, 'This is bullshit.'" she said.

Instead of letting her frustration boil over, Dom used it to fuel her improvement in subsequent challenges. She maintained a positive perspective, knowing that staying safe each week meant she remained on the show while others were sent home. Eventually, Heidi Klum announced that Dom was one of the five designers who would create a collection for New York Fashion Week. This led to a home visit from Tim Gunn, twelve hectic weeks of work, and the biggest runway show of her life. Dom became the first Black woman to win *Project Runway*.

After the show, Dom returned to normal life, focusing on motherhood while creating at home. This fulfilling experience eventually led her to work for Urban Outfitters, giving her insight into the corporate design side of the fashion industry.

She came to the realization that she preferred the autonomy of working for herself. "I'm grateful for my time with Urban Outfitters and other companies," Dom said. "But designing for someone else means adhering to schedules, deadlines, and various teams. Working for yourself allows more flexibility and autonomy. You can pause, reevaluate, and make better creative decisions."

Dom's decision to bet on herself paid off when she was invited to compete on *Project Runway All Stars*. Her unshakeable calm and bold prints helped her win, placing her among elite designers and earning $100,000 in prize money, a complete studio, and a shoe collection deal. She invested her winnings in an apartment-studio space in West Philadelphia, close to where her creative journey began.

While active on social media, Dom avoids cheap gimmicks, preferring to build a following through quality work. "I like to play the long game," Dom said. "I'd rather earn followers with great work than gain them from gimmicks. Many streamers and YouTubers imitate those who gamed the algorithm without good content. I have no interest in that."

MASTERING MULTIPLE MEDIUMS

A recurrent theme among the creators in this book is that while they excel in their primary pursuits, they also push themselves to be proficient in other art forms. Dom deliberately takes breaks from fashion design to explore her passion for other creative outlets.

"I've run a business. I've worked in the industry for over a decade," Dom said. "I've done *Project Runway*. I had to take a step back during the pandemic and do a little self-reflection. I asked myself, 'Are you interested in doing anything else?' I decided I just wanted to paint, so I went back to where I originally was as an artist when I was younger. It was a nice palate cleanser. Especially in terms of textile design, I had a new start."

Another way Dom is doing things differently is by offering a direct-to-consumer model. Many designers aim to get their clothing into boutiques, which creates waste and eats into profit margins. In contrast, Dom creates her own patterns and only incorporates them into a garment when a customer places an order via her website. One of two companies she carefully selected produces just enough fabric for her in-house seamstress to construct the finished product. This approach allows her to pay a living wage and uphold her core value of environmental responsibility.

"I decided that I'm only going to make clothes when a consumer says they really want to own them," Dom said. "And if it messes up the bottom line for me and I don't make as much money, that's fine. At least I'll be able to live with myself, know that I'm not being wasteful, and be content that the people who buy my designs are going to appreciate them."

While working for fashion brands, Dom traveled all over Asia and saw how mass-market clothing is produced. These experiences opened her eyes to the exploitation prevalent in the industry and solidified her conviction to do things differently.

"Going abroad to see how clothes are made and what daily working conditions in factories actually look like led me to take more of an empathetic approach in my creative process," Dom said. "I take care of my seamstress, and if I hire someone else to help with a collection, I can pay them at least a livable wage. And then on top of that, I consider what else I can do to make their lives easier so they can give me the best work possible. Because otherwise, what's the point?"

To set a firm foundation for her own artistry, the teamwork she instills in her collaborators, and how she parents her daughter, Dom sticks to a solid daily routine.

"I wake up every morning at five and go watch the sunrise," Dom said. "There's something really nice and magical about that time of the day where no one bothers you. There are no phone calls. You don't have to email. Nobody's awake. There's a sense of stillness and quiet to just be. Then I go work in increments of half an hour at a time, followed by a five-minute break. When I hit a roadblock, I have to walk away for a while. I always bring a book with me because sometimes I might wind up at the park and I'll sit down and read for a little bit or people watch. Then I get back to it."

Dom also thinks back to the times when she'd try out different creative mediums as a teenager looking to find herself. She believes that taking a creative break to practice another art form can provide much-needed mental relief, particularly after getting into a cognitively demanding flow state with textile design.

"I practice ballet a couple of times a week and always look forward to it," she said. "I also learned to love music at a young age because of my dad. There's so much about the creative process that's under the surface. It's like a duck swimming on water—you don't see the feet moving. Depending on the type of creativity that you're involved in, your respite might look different. Because I participate in the visual arts and am sit-ting here at my desk with a tablet, sketching on paper, or doing 3D design on my computer, having something in the physical or performing arts to fall back on helps a lot."

⚡ CREATIVE SPARKS 5 ⚡

Embrace "creative breaks" like Dom. Can activities such as paint-ing, music, or dance ignite fresh inspiration in your core artistic pursuit? Explore diverse outlets to fuel your creativity and nour-ish your artistic spirit. Remember, a well-rounded life fosters a sustainable creative practice that thrives.

FROM PROTÉGÉ TO MENTOR

One of the most enjoyable aspects of researching this chapter was dis-covering a YouTube video of a Moore College *Project Runway* watch party. The tension was palpable as the season twelve finale concluded, with stu-dents eagerly awaiting Heidi Klum's announcement of the winner. When she said, "Dom, congratulations, you are the winner of *Project Runway*," the room erupted in joyous celebration. To give back to these students, Dom returned to Moore College, assuming a mentorship and teaching role similar to Tim Gunn's.

"I found teaching intriguing because they were me in that moment," Dom said. "I had to think about how I felt in their shoes, understand how they were approaching their art, and get them to look at it from a differ-ent perspective. They can get hung up on the notion that they need to make money in fashion. You can't be a starving artist because you have to stay alive to create, but if you do it for yourself and you're satisfied, then eff it—nothing else matters."

When advising students, whether at her alma mater or responding to online inquiries, Dom emphasizes avoiding the comparison trap. "I get worried about the internet because there's so much mimicry and not a lot of originality. Companies try to get in on every trend, instead of creating to meet a real demand or setting a new direction. To me, that's really frustrating."

Dom offers young designers practical advice on combining hand-drawn sketches with three-dimensional renderings, printing their own textiles on demand, and working with an in-house seamstress—all elements of her business she has mastered in recent years. Her guidance also centers on mindset and self-reflection.

"Know yourself," Dom said. "Know who you are and what you like before you attach yourself to any one idea. Becoming aware of what type of artist or creative person you want to be is the most important first step. If you don't know who you are, then how can you possibly make an aesthetic decision?"

She encourages young designers to embrace their individuality and focus on self-awareness. "Learn how you respond to the rules, how you work, and how you behave, and then you'll develop your own spirit and aesthetic. You can't do this without having first established where you are mentally and creatively," Dom said.

With the abundance of hacks promoted on social media, in books, and on podcasts, young creators can become impatient when they realize they can't take shortcuts to mastery. Dom preaches patience to the young designers she mentors. "There's this expectation as a creative that you're going to be perfect at something immediately," Dom said. "You might just need a little bit more time than other people take, and there's nothing wrong with that."

"I don't think we give ourselves enough grace in our day-to-day lives to be human, have learning curves, mess up, and make mistakes. Why are you trying to be perfect? There's no such thing. So stop."

Dom's message to aspiring creatives is clear: embrace imperfection and, as a Tim Gunn catch phrase suggests, carry on. "Just keep taking the shots that matter because if you don't, nothing will happen. If you shoot and miss, then at least you know. I've learned to have a little faith and go from there. Things will work out for you."

✄ **CREATIVE SPARKS 6** ✄

Dom's journey encourages us to embrace our individuality. Self-reflection unlocks your artistic core. How can self-awareness and a relentless pursuit of originality help you develop your unique style and shine brightly in your creative field?

THE 5 Cs IN DOM STREATER'S JOURNEY

Dom Streater's remarkable journey of becoming a two-time *Project Runway* winner embodies the essence of mental toughness through the 5 Cs:

1. **Courage:** Dom's journey began in a financially challenged background, where she learned sewing out of necessity. This adversity instilled in her the courage to pursue fashion despite limited resources and societal expectations. Her decision to pursue a spot on *Project Runway* after an initial rejection highlights her bravery and readiness to face critiques and competition.

2. **Confidence:** Dom's confidence is evident in her bold designs and unique style. Her willingness to take risks and experiment with new techniques allowed her to create captivating pieces that stood out in the fashion world. This self-assurance in her creative instincts was pivotal in distinguishing her during competitions on *Project Runway*.

3. **Concentration:** On *Project Runway*, Dom's ability to concentrate under tight deadlines and intense pressure was crucial to her win. She managed her time effectively and focused intensely on her designs, employing a methodical approach to sketching, draping, and constructing each garment, which ensured her consistent performance.

4. **Composure:** Dom's composure under pressure was a key

aspect of her mental toughness. Facing judges' critiques and competitive tensions on *Project Runway*, she remained poised and professional, keeping her goals in sharp focus amid the chaos, which was vital for her success.

5. **Commitment:** Dom's commitment to her craft was evident through late-night sewing sessions and a continuous drive for excellence. Her dedication distinguished her path to success on *Project Runway* and continued to inspire her even after her victories, fueling her ongoing commitment to innovation and growth.

YOUR CREATIVE TOOLKIT

Just as Dom Streater exemplifies the 5 Cs of mental toughness in her journey as a two-time *Project Runway* winner, you too can develop these strengths. Here are practical tips and tools based on the 5 Cs of creativity, inspired by her journey.

1. **Courage:**
   - **Unleash Your Bold Hero:** Define your bold self by imagining an alter ego that embodies courage. Are they audacious and flamboyant, or do they possess quiet strength and unwavering focus? This alter ego isn't a fake; it's a way to tap into and amplify your inner bravery. Think of Beyoncé channeling "Sasha Fierce" to enhance her stage presence and performance.
   - **Embody Your Brave Identity:** Express your alter ego through your appearance. Does your creative persona favor bold colors, a minimalist aesthetic, or a stylish hat? Use these external flourishes to embody your alter ego's confidence and creativity.
   - **Dance with Your Courageous Self:** Let your courageous alter ego lead you into bold action, guiding you as you embrace your creative flow and take charge of your artistic

vision. Use this transformation to fuel your creativity and
push your boundaries.

2. **Confidence:**
   - **Visualize Your Victory:** Visualize success and channel belief
     in your craft. Focus on positive thoughts and vivid success
     visualizations to connect with your true potential. Embrace
     the mindset that you are already the successful creative you
     aspire to be.
   - **Exude Confidence:** Adopt the "Act As If" mindset by
     embodying confidence. Enter situations with an assured
     presence, a bright smile, and positive body language,
     amplifying your genuine qualities. Acting "As If" isn't
     pretending; it's drawing out your inherent potential.
   - **Command Your Presence:** Maintain eye contact, stand tall
     with your shoulders back, and offer a firm handshake. By
     projecting confidence outwardly, you'll reinforce your inner
     belief in your creative abilities, helping you to own your
     unique voice and artistic vision.

3. **Concentration:**
   - **Mental Focus Drill 1:** Start at 100 and count backward,
     subtracting by sixes. This keeps your mind active and
     improves your ability to concentrate on intricate details.
     Repeat this exercise with a different starting number
     regularly as a fun way to build concentration.
   - **Mental Focus Drill 2:** Begin at 150 and count backward,
     subtracting by eights. This variation challenges your brain to
     handle complex tasks with sustained attention. Repeat this
     exercise with a different starting number regularly as a fun
     way to build concentration.
   - **Mental Focus Drill 3:** Start at 200 and count backward,
     subtracting by sevens. This mentally stimulating
     exercise sharpens your focus. Repeat this exercise with a
     different starting number regularly as a fun way to build
     concentration.

4. **Composure:**
    - **Navigate with Calm Curiosity:** When emotions run high and judgment feels clouded, get curious. Ask yourself, "What can I learn from this challenge?" or "How can I approach this from a new perspective?" Remind yourself, "Calm curiosity reveals new possibilities."
    - **Embrace Curiosity in Stalled Moments:** If you hit a creative block, rather than getting stuck, shift your mindset to curiosity. Tell yourself, "I'm curious about what comes next," and open up to new possibilities.
    - **Let Curiosity Lead:** In moments of uncertainty or self-doubt, let curiosity be your compass. Say to yourself, "Curiosity leads, creativity follows," and use that mindset to guide your next steps.

5. **Commitment:**
    - **Build Your Bridge:** Success is built one plank at a time, each representing a small, consistent effort. Lay each plank with intention, knowing the collective work forms a sturdy, reliable path. Don't get discouraged by single steps—focus on the bigger picture. Stay committed, and plank by plank, you'll build the bridge to your goals.
    - **Add Planks with Purpose:** Each plank strengthens your bridge. Like a master engineer, ensure every effort is intentional and aligned with your vision. Trust the process, knowing that every step brings you closer to your goal.
    - **Envision Your Completed Crossing:** Keep your eyes on the finished bridge. Picture the pride of standing on the other side, knowing your dedication has connected you to your dreams. Let this vision fuel your commitment, even when the journey feels long. Every plank moves you closer to solid ground.

IN THE NEXT CHAPTER

Witness the brilliance of Stephen Wiltshire, where photographic memory meets architectural artistry. Discover how Stephen's extraordinary ability to re-create entire cityscapes from memory has made him a celebrated artist worldwide, offering profound lessons in dedication and creative genius.

Chapter 10

THE POWER OF PEN AND PAPER: STEPHEN WILTSHIRE

The expansive canvas seems boundless, stretching out endlessly. At one end, a young man sits on a white stool. With big black AKG headphones perched on his head, he bends forward, intent on adding another line to this work in progress. As he draws a window on the side of the towering New York skyscraper, he contentedly hums along with his music's melody, one part of his prodigious mind lost in sound while another prompts his right hand to reproduce the cityscape in precise detail. A smile, a slight flick of the wrist, and the first building is complete. Now for the rest of the Big Apple's skyline.

This particular chapter of Stephen Wiltshire's life finds him serving as an inspiration to people worldwide, the focus of his own gallery in London, and the subject of a captivating documentary. But as that film reveals, Stephen's story began with some major obstacles. He was diagnosed with autism at the age of three and didn't say his first words until he was five. Fittingly, they were "paper" and "pencil"—just like Pablo Picasso.

Despite his early struggles with spoken language, Stephen found another way to communicate. He drew nature scenes, caricatures of his teachers at Queensmill School in London, and buildings. Seeking to develop Stephen's gift, his older sister, Annette, took him around London to find settings that he could add to his sketchbooks, which were filling up fast. Soon his precocious talent started gaining media attention, and when Stephen was eight years old, former prime minister Edward Heath commissioned him to draw Salisbury Cathedral. Soon after, Sir Hugh Casson, president of the Royal Academy of Art, called him "Britain's best childhood artist."

FROM STRUGGLES TO MASTERPIECES

Five years later, Stephen collected some of his favorite creations into a book, aptly titled *Drawings*. Inspired by his love of urban landscapes, Stephen released *Cities* two years later. His third book, *Floating Cities*, reached number one on the *Sunday Times* bestseller list. He later honed his natural talent with expert instruction at City and Guilds of London Art School, graduating with a postgraduate degree in drawing and printmaking.

No matter how complex his drawings have become as he has matured into the world's premier architectural artist, it's Stephen's simple joy that keeps him coming back renewed, refreshed, and enthused every time he picks up his pen again. "I feel great," Stephen said. "I feel happy about it while I'm drawing because it makes me feel good and relaxed." His remarkable attention to detail and extraordinary ability to re-create entire cityscapes from memory never fail to amaze and inspire audiences worldwide.

Stephen's artwork transcends technical skill, embodying the profound passion and dedication he pours into each creation. Far from being defined by his autism diagnosis and the initial challenges he faced, Stephen has an ability to turn his unique way of seeing the world into breathtakingly detailed drawings, which has made him a celebrated artist.

The joy and tranquility he finds in his work are palpable, drawing viewers into his world with every stroke of his pen. Stephen's art serves as a reminder of the incredible potential within all individuals, regardless of the challenges they may face, and his story continues to inspire countless others to pursue their passions with unwavering dedication.

✎ CREATIVE SPARKS 1 ✎

Consider what creative spark ignites you. Are there talents or passions you've overlooked or haven't fully explored? Take a moment to reflect on activities that might bring you the same kind of joy and relaxation that Stephen feels when he draws.

SEEING THE WORLD THROUGH STEPHEN'S EYES

Many know Stephen Wiltshire for his drawings of famous London landmarks like St. Paul's Cathedral, Big Ben, and the Houses of Parliament. Some of his most iconic illustrations also feature British cultural artifacts, such as distinctive double-decker buses, black cabs, and red phone boxes. While his fans remain captivated by his portrayals of England, Stephen has also sought inspiration abroad.

In 2005, he took his second trip to Tokyo, where he created his largest panorama to date. Later that year, he delighted Italian fans by faithfully re-creating St. Peter's Basilica and the Vatican as part of a drawing of Rome. After viewing Hong Kong's Victoria Harbor from the air for only twenty minutes, Stephen completed a thirty-foot drawing of the view. In 2014, he spent two days drawing the Singapore cityscape from memory at the Paragon mall, and 150,000 visitors flocked to the widescreen canvas within the first five days.

While Stephen has found joy in visiting countries around the world, America holds a special place in his heart and portfolio. For his fourth book, *Stephen Wiltshire's American Dream*, he made three trips across the Atlantic with his literary agent, Margaret Hewson. He meticulously captured the cityscapes of Los Angeles; Washington, DC; and Chicago—home to the first skyscraper—in extraordinary detail, contrasting them with the natural beauty of the Grand Canyon. Stephen and Annette have since returned to the U.S. many times, with one city in particular always offering him something new to draw.

"New York City is my favorite—the energy and electricity," Stephen said. "It has tall buildings, skyscrapers, avenues, yellow New York taxis, and crowds of people."

Stephen has faithfully re-created all of these landmarks in his illustrations of the city. His admiration for the Big Apple is reciprocated. When the Empire State Building unveiled its redesigned eightieth-floor observatory in 2019, Stephen's 2017 city panorama was prominently featured. UBS commissioned him to create a drawing of Manhattan, which was displayed as a 250-foot-long poster at John F. Kennedy International Airport. Additionally, in New York City, Stephen drew a twenty-foot canvas live on CBS, a task that took five days. The stunning results demonstrated Stephen's persistence in the face of fatigue. "Sometimes my hand gets tired, but I always keep going because I work hard," he said.

One of the remarkable aspects of Stephen's work is the juxtaposition of expansive panoramas with intricate details. Following just one helicopter ride over a city, Stephen can re-create its buildings from memory with astonishing accuracy, down to the number of floors. This incredible skill inspired the title of a critically acclaimed documentary about him: *Billions of Windows.* Flying above a location gives Stephen a unique perspective that he later brings to life when he sits down to draw. His love of flight underscores the importance of awe and inspiration for artists.

"I'm excited to see the landmarks, the city's skyscrapers, and the views," Stephen said. "It's so beautiful from up there."

As cameras record Stephen creating several stunningly detailed drawings, the cityscapes his pen brings to life change from moment to moment. Yet one constant is his lineup of black headphones and white earbuds. While his illustrations may seem effortless, they require recalling each detail from his astonishing memory and re-creating it on paper or canvas with unbroken concentration. Stephen needs to block out distractions to find and stay in a flow state.

"Music helps me to concentrate while I'm drawing," Stephen said. "I love to listen to 1970s disco, sixties and seventies Motown, and soul music."

Among his go-to artists are Kool & the Gang, the Bee Gees, the Jackson Five, and Earth, Wind & Fire, with Ben E. King's "Stand by Me" and Sam Cooke's "Wonderful World" remaining firm favorites on an ever-expanding playlist.

⁄ CREATIVE SPARKS 2 ⁄

Stephen's unique perspective transforms bustling cityscapes into intricate works of art. His ability to capture the essence of a place by noticing even the tiniest details is remarkable. Think about the beauty that surrounds you daily. What small things do you overlook when rushing through life? How can you slow down to truly see and appreciate the world around you?

THE CRAFT BEHIND THE ART

Imagine Stephen standing before a panoramic canvas nearly the size of a movie theater screen. Just a few days ago, it was blank. Minute by minute, line by line, hour by hour, he has transformed it into a vibrant representation of Singapore, Sydney, or his hometown of London. Stephen finds immense pleasure, satisfaction, and intrinsic motivation in the meticulous process of creating something unique from scratch, in a way only he can. Beyond the joy of creation, Stephen revels in the reactions of others to his work, the smiles and wide eyes of those who marvel at his intricate cityscapes and landscapes.

"It makes me happy and excited to see their reactions," Stephen said. "It means a lot to me that people like seeing my work, and it's a lot of fun when I get asked to draw for someone."

Many assume elite artists capture lightning in a bottle, overlooking the vital importance of consistency in their process. While each piece of Stephen's artwork is a testament to his genius, it is his disciplined and regular routine that enables him to transform a blank page into some of the world's most intricate and precise drawings. Interestingly, Stephen sketches more people than buildings, but these personal portraits remain private, not intended for public display.

"I draw in my sketchbook, making ideas at home and in the studio at my gallery," Stephen noted. "Sometimes I go out and draw new sights in the book. That feels exciting."

Even as his art has progressed over the years and he has taken on more ambitious drawings, the main tool of Stephen's trade remains constant. "I use the same Staedtler pens for every drawing," Stephen said. Specifically, Stephen utilizes 0.5 and 0.7 mm Staedtler pigment liners to put fine details down on premium Daler-Rowney or Hahnemühle drawing paper. When filling out the thousands of details on a panorama, Stephen has to have a large stock of his signature pens on hand to make sure he doesn't run out partway through the project.

"Depending on where the work is situated, the air can dry out the pigment very quickly, so Stephen goes through pens very fast," his sister Annette said. By the end of one of his most ambitious projects, he might have used up four or five boxes. Having a ready supply of consistent materials helps Stephen avoid decision fatigue and focus more on his drawing.

While Stephen's gift is arguably one of a kind and his vision unique, his art did not develop in isolation. Rather, he has looked to some of the masters in hyperrealism to inspire his viewpoint and how he develops his already expansive portfolio. "Richard Estes is my favorite because he paints landscapes, cities, gates, street scenes, buildings, and cars," Stephen shared. "It's realistic with very detailed colors, and all on canvas."

For many years, Stephen stuck to the monochrome drawings that his trademark black pen is so well suited to and known for. But while many of his illustrations are still in black and white, an iconic piece of British design inspired him to evolve aesthetically and extend the range of his portfolio.

"He started using color for red double-decker buses," Annette explained. "They're pretty much phased out now, so it brings back memories for our generation and older people. That kind of detail makes the drawings stand out, and people really connect to them."

After infusing red into buses, Stephen did likewise with yellow for New York taxis and the Big Ben clockface, blue for the River Thames, and green for Centre Court at Wimbledon. "Color mixing seemed like a good idea for buses, taxis, trees, rivers, and the sky," Stephen remarked. To add different tones and shades to his drawing, Stephen has augmented his usual Staedtler pens with colored pastels and sometimes even oil paints. Willing to experiment with different styles and materials, he also introduces shading using pencils when needed.

Athletes often use visualization to rehearse shooting free throws, kicking field goals, or running races. Similarly, some artists utilize mental imagery to conjure their next masterpiece in their mind before turning it into reality. Mental imagery is a key component of Stephen's approach. "I always dream about my art. I've seen Canary Wharf, the City of London, Tower Bridge, and the New York skyline," Stephen said. After such a dream, "I often draw it straight away." Other times, he pulls from memories of London landmarks from years before.

⚡ CREATIVE SPARKS 3 ⚡

Stephen's dedication highlights the importance of routine, quality tools, and experimentation. What small changes can you make to optimize your creative environment? Reflect on how you can incorporate consistent practices and high-quality materials into your creative process.

INSPIRING FUTURE ARTISTS

In 2006, Queen Elizabeth II honored Stephen with an MBE (Member of the Order of the British Empire) for his contributions to art. Later that year, with the support of Annette and her husband, Zoltan, Stephen opened a permanent gallery in the picturesque Royal Opera Arcade in London, which was designed by Regency architect John Nash and is the oldest example of its kind. Bathed in sunlight from circular skylights and with tile floors underfoot, it was the perfect venue to showcase Stephen's work to visitors from around the world.

Stephen has since moved to a more spacious gallery in Chelsea Harbour, offering a place for collectors to meet him and view his latest editions by appointment. This gallery, which Stephen affectionately calls his "pad," also serves as a creative space where he can think and sketch.

Stephen's work has left an indelible mark not only on London but also on numerous other locations worldwide. More importantly, his boundless creativity continues to inspire children who meet him at special appearances, eagerly line up to see him during his travels, or watch his art evolve from afar. Annette has witnessed firsthand the profound impact Stephen's art has on the next generation, as well as on the parents and teachers who use his story as a case study for what's possible when one pursues their passion.

"Stephen has a center named after him in London called the Stephen Wiltshire Centre," Annette said. "It's a play-off from the original special needs school that he used to go to in Fulham. Many other schools in the UK and worldwide have opened art classrooms named the Stephen Wiltshire Room or the Stephen Wiltshire Art Class. We're inundated every week with young creatives who want to be inspired by watching the way Stephen works and use him as a step forward in progressing their talent. It's always very humbling."

Stephen finds motivation in the gratitude he feels toward his fans for appreciating his artwork. He is particularly moved by the feedback from children and hopes his drawings inspire them to cultivate their own creativity.

"It means a lot to me because people say, 'He's talented, he's good, and he's doing his best,'" Stephen said. "I feel supported, and it makes me happy that they enjoy my work."

Stephen also touches the lives of those with family members or friends who have special needs. Annette has seen how Stephen's artwork and his consistently positive demeanor have provided hope to many.

"Sometimes people are crying," Annette said. "They feel like they can connect to him, especially when they have siblings who are on the spectrum and feel there's no help or way forward. Then they see someone like Stephen, who's been through many hurdles throughout his life and doesn't show people that he's been troubled. He's very relaxed and humble about everything that he does."

⚟ CREATIVE SPARKS 4 ⚟

Stephen's journey demonstrates the power of creativity to inspire and impact others. How can you leverage your talents to positively influence the world? Does your creativity empower others? Can your work spread joy, hope, or connection? Consider how your creativity can leave a lasting mark.

THE POWER OF PARTNERSHIP

Stephen's enduring success stems from harnessing and refining his extraordinary natural talents, significantly aided by his collaboration with Annette, who serves as his art director, and her husband, Zoltan, who manages his gallery.

The siblings have worked together since Annette was thirteen and Stephen was ten, forming a lasting partnership that allows Stephen to concentrate fully on sketching, drawing, and exploring new source material. Over the years, Annette has observed how Stephen's art has transformed lives, and she believes his resilient mindset and determined attitude are just as inspiring as his artwork itself.

"When I'm down or I'm feeling low, I look at my brother from a distance and it reminds me not to give up," Annette said. "You just continue going because that's what life is about: to be happy and to look forward. This is what I say to everybody. He's very passionate about his work, and he sees the rewards from it by how people relate to him and how they love his art. My brother is my inspiration because throughout everything we've gone through, he has never complained once. Even if you secretly film him, he's got this permanent smile in his eyes and on his face. He's happy, regardless of the conditions that have been bestowed on him. I find that anybody who can do that is a very strong individual. I look up to people like that."

Whether it's an adult rekindling their passion for art, a classroom of children needing encouragement to display their drawings, or a TV audience of millions seeking creative inspiration, Stephen's work has had a truly global impact. He exemplifies that everyone has a unique talent that might not be immediately apparent, but with persistent nurturing, this can flourish into something extraordinary.

When asked what advice he would give to other creators, Stephen offered simple yet profound guidance: "Do the best you can and never stop."

✔ CREATIVE SPARKS 5 ✔

Collaboration is essential in creative endeavors. How can partnering with others help you focus on your strengths and achieve your goals? What kind of support do you need to thrive creatively? Reflect on the benefits of having a supportive team or partner and consider how they can enhance your creative journey.

THE 5 Cs IN STEPHEN WILTSHIRE'S JOURNEY

Stephen Wiltshire's remarkable journey and his artistic prowess unveil the power of the 5 Cs:

1. **Courage:** Stephen's artistic journey showcases boldness and resilience. Diagnosed with autism early in life and despite

having challenges with the spoken language, he leverages his unique perspective to create complex cityscapes from memory, embodying courage with every sketch.

2. **Confidence:** Stephen's confidence in his artistic abilities allows him to undertake monumental projects. His talent for capturing detailed panoramas has brought him international recognition, affirming that self-belief can elevate exceptional skills to create masterpieces.

3. **Concentration:** Known for his intense focus, Stephen meticulously renders architectural details, often while listening to his favorite music. This concentration enables him to exclude distractions and achieve a high level of precision in his work.

4. **Composure:** Facing high expectations, Stephen remains calm and collected, using his artistry to channel his emotions. His ability to maintain composure, whether drawing live on television or from memory, allows him to produce inspiring works.

5. **Commitment:** Demonstrating unwavering dedication, Stephen's commitment to his art is evident in his continuous pursuit of excellence. He consistently chooses high-quality materials and explores new techniques, showing a profound dedication to evolving his craft.

YOUR CREATIVE TOOLKIT

Just as Stephen Wiltshire exemplifies the 5 Cs of mental toughness in his journey as an architectural artist, you too can develop these strengths. Here are practical tips and tools based on the 5 Cs of creativity, inspired by his journey.

1. **Courage:**
    -   **Unleash Your Inner Daredevil:** Creative growth is fueled by calculated risks. Take the leap and embark on a new project or experiment with an untested idea. Remember,

uncertainty and potential failure are the sparks that ignite the fire of innovation, propelling you forward. What small risk can you take today to ignite a creative spark?

- **Bravery in Small, Steady Steps:** Fear gradually fades as progress unfolds. Start with manageable creative goals, methodically chipping away at fear and boosting confidence with each step forward. Celebrate small victories and watch momentum build. Identify one bite-sized creative goal you can tackle today and get started.

- **Find Freedom in Imperfection:** Mistakes are an inherent and valuable part of the creative journey. By accepting imperfections, you'll feel empowered to experiment more boldly, unencumbered by the fear of failure. This mindset unlocks new creative possibilities and fosters growth. Affirm to yourself: "I am brave enough to learn from my mistakes and evolve through creative challenges."

2. **Confidence:**
   - **Tackle Perfectionism:** Challenge perfectionistic thoughts with positive, realistic ones. Shift from "I must be flawless" to "I am doing my best, and that's something to be proud of." This reframing fosters a growth mindset. When self-doubt creeps in, counter it with: "I trust myself and my abilities, and I celebrate my efforts!"

   - **Counter Negativity:** Catch and counter negativity from yourself or others. Acknowledge negative thoughts or comments, then respond with a balanced perspective. Reframe "I'll never finish this project" to a more empowering statement like "I'm making progress, one step at a time, and that's progress worth celebrating." Identify a negative thought or comment today and reframe it into a positive statement that motivates you.

   - **Celebrate Your Wins:** Regularly acknowledge and celebrate your accomplishments, big or small. This reinforces a positive self-image and boosts confidence. Take a moment each day to recognize your successes. Say to yourself, "I honor my achievements and proudly celebrate my growth and progress!"

3. **Concentration:**
   - **Integrate Ego and Instinct:** Balance planning with creative impulses by staying focused and present in the moment. Listen to both your rational thoughts and intuitive feelings. How can you better integrate both logic and intuition in your creative process today?
   - **Get in the Laser-Focus Zone:** Create a distraction-free zone, your personal creative sanctuary where distractions bounce off as if it is a superhero deflecting attacks. This is where your most epic ideas will emerge. What's one thing you can do today to create a more distraction-free creative space?
   - **Build Your Creative Muscle:** Start with short bursts of focused work, like twenty-five minutes of zero distractions, followed by a break. Gradually increase your focus time, building concentration like muscle memory. Challenge yourself: How can you incorporate a twenty-five-minute focused work session into your schedule this week?

4. **Composure:**
   - **Cultivate Self-Compassion:** Remember, you're part of a shared human experience where everyone faces challenges and makes mistakes. When you stumble, remind yourself that you're not alone and that it's okay not to be perfect. Say: "I'm doing the best I can, and that's enough. I'm part of a larger community that struggles and learns together. I trust in my basic goodness and know that I'm fundamentally okay, no matter what." This mindset allows you to approach difficulties with kindness, understanding, and patience.
   - **Follow the Three-Second Rule:** When emotions run high, pause for three seconds before reacting. Ask yourself: "What response aligns with my values and integrity?" or "How do I want to show up in this moment?" This brief pause helps you respond thoughtfully instead of reacting impulsively.

- **Shift to Gratitude:** When you catch yourself complaining or focusing on what's lacking, you're likely tuned in to the *Entitlement Channel*—fixated on what you feel you're owed or expect. To shift your mindset, switch to the *Gratitude Channel* by reflecting on three things you genuinely appreciate about your current situation. This shift will help you regain perspective and approach challenges with a more positive mindset.

5. **Commitment:**
   - **Kickstart Your Creative Day:** Jumpstart your day with creative fire! Pick one action that'll move the needle on your goals—whether it's sketching out ideas, brainstorming, or just diving in. Make the most of your creative journey today—no time to waste, let's go!
   - **Turn Challenges into Power-Ups:** Think of challenges as creative power-ups! That task you dread? It's a secret level to unlock hidden skills and level up. Pick one tough task today and reframe it as a chance to grow stronger in your craft.
   - **Celebrate Sacrifices as Wins:** Sacrifices are the fuel for your creative rocket. Every tough choice pushes you closer to mastery. Take a moment to celebrate a recent sacrifice you've made for your craft—it's proof of your commitment and growth!

IN THE NEXT CHAPTER

Enter the realm of Erik Larson, where rigorous research and captivating storytelling converge. Learn how his unique blend of historical accuracy and narrative flair has catapulted him to bestselling author status. We'll delve into the secrets behind his success and the creative discipline that sets him apart.

Chapter 11

THE STORYTELLER'S CRAFT: ERIK LARSON

An autumn mist gathers around the historian as he flips up his coat collar to ward off the cold. Stepping off the sidewalk onto the cobbled street, he begins to see what Winston Churchill saw all those years ago when the fate of freedom and democracy hung in the balance. Retracing the resilient prime minister's steps, he envisions the jutting jaw, the tapping cane, and the homburg hat as Churchill made his way from the Houses of Parliament to the nerve center of Britain's battle against Hitler: the Cabinet War Rooms. Later, when he sits down to write, the historian will conjure all the telling details of these walks, transporting his readers back to wartime London.

Some artists follow a predictable career path, gradually advancing in a specific niche until they achieve their dream role. Others take a more circuitous route, using experiences from several related disciplines to build a diverse skill set that equips them to seize unforeseen opportunities. *New York Times* bestselling author Erik Larson falls into the latter category.

After earning a master's degree from Columbia University's prestigious School of Journalism and cutting his cub reporter's teeth at the *Bucks County Courier Times*, Erik landed a gig that any young journalist would envy: staff writer for *The Wall Street Journal*. This was during what could be called the last Golden Age of feature writing before storytelling morphed into "content" and investigative reporting took a back seat to clicks, views, and retweets. At the *WSJ*, Erik was given free rein to hone his researching, interviewing, and reporting skills.

AN UNPREDICTABLE PATH TO SUCCESS

Rather than settling into a secure, long-term role at a renowned news-paper, Erik chose a different path. When his wife accepted a position at the Johns Hopkins Hospital in Baltimore, he resigned from *The Wall Street Journal* and joined her, a decision that brought him to a professional crossroads. For the first time in years, Erik was uncertain about his next steps. He wanted to continue writing but felt disillusioned with the newspaper industry. This prompted him to pivot dramatically and start writing a "literate detective novel," though it remains unpublished.

Despite the novel's incompletion, the shift was significant. It marked Erik's departure from the conventional trajectory of a journalist to exploring the broader realm of writing. Soon enough, he began to miss the structure and challenge of features, which led him back to magazine writing. One of his early pitches to *Time* magazine was accepted, and he quickly became a regular contributor. This opportunity opened doors to writing for esteemed publications like *The Atlantic, The New Yorker*, and *Harper's*.

"I realized that, for all the work I was putting into a long magazine piece, I might as well be doing books," Erik said. "And books would last on the shelf a whole lot longer." This realization was pivotal. It wasn't just about the length of his work but the lasting impact he desired to achieve. Books, unlike articles, had the potential to stay relevant and be revisited by readers for years to come.

The courage to deviate from a predictable path often distinguishes great creators from the rest. Erik's willingness to leave behind a prestigious position and embrace uncertainty allowed him to explore various facets of writing and ultimately discover his true calling in narrative nonfiction. His journey underscores the importance of following one's instincts and being open to change, even when it involves significant risk.

Success is not always immediate. Erik's initial foray into novel writing did not yield the results he hoped for, but it was a crucial step in his creative evolution. It taught him valuable lessons and helped him refine his focus. This willingness to experiment and pivot is a common thread among successful creators. They understand that each experience, whether successful or not, adds to their repertoire of skills and insights, ultimately enriching their primary pursuits. By continuously seeking new challenges, embracing change, and reinventing himself, Erik exemplifies how taking risks and remaining adaptable can lead to profound personal and professional growth.

✏ CREATIVE SPARKS 1 ✏

Erik's journey shows that success is not always a straight path. Reflect on how diverse experiences can enrich your creative growth. What new skills can you explore to enhance your main pursuits? Take on that project you've been hesitating to start—it might lead you to unexpected opportunities.

A LASTING LEGACY

Though he would eventually pen a second unpublished novel, Erik recognized that his true talent lay in nonfiction. In 1992, he published his first book, *The Naked Consumer*, which exposed how companies invade consumers' privacy by selling their information. This book demonstrated the same diligent reporting and narrative flair as his articles, foreshadowing the assault on privacy that social media companies would later mount. Reflecting on its reception, Erik later remarked, "I loved that book. No one else did."

Despite *The Naked Consumer*'s lack of commercial success, it proved to Erik that he was capable of writing longform works. "This was hard, but I was happy," he said. Bitten by the book bug, Erik released another investigative title, *Lethal Passage*, two years later. It explored America's gun culture and the devastating consequences that shootings wreak upon families and communities.

As satisfied as he was by diligent fact-finding, Erik again changed his creative course after completing *Lethal Passage*. While an undergraduate at the University of Pennsylvania, he'd studied Russian history, language, and culture, and decided to combine his curiosity about the past with his reporter's eye for telling details in subsequent narrative nonfiction books. The first was *Isaac's Storm*, the story of the devastating hurricane that struck Galveston, Texas, in 1900. *The Washington Post* called it "the *Jaws* of hurricane yarns," and it landed Erik on several Book of the Year lists.

Erik's second historical book, *The Devil in the White City*, is a dual narrative that intertwines the horrifying crimes of serial killer H. H. Holmes with the tale of architect Daniel Burnham's preparations for the 1893 Chicago World's Fair. Quickly becoming Erik's second-straight *New York Times* bestseller, the book also garnered an Edgar Award for fact-based crime writing.

In subsequent works, Erik turned his talents to diverse historical topics: the invention of wireless radio transmission in *Thunderstruck*, the sinking of the Lusitania in *Dead Wake*, and the experiences of the U.S. ambassador to Nazi Germany in *In the Garden of Beasts*. In all of these, Erik showcased his rare gift for zooming out to capture the big picture while vividly re-creating the lives of his protagonists and the bygone worlds they inhabited.

For someone like Erik, whose historical interests span centuries and transcend national borders, there's a potentially infinite supply of stories to corral into compelling microcosm narratives. Yet he recognizes that whether he comes up with an idea or it's given to him by a friend, family member, or fan, not every notion is book-worthy and most have to be discarded, particularly given the commitment that each new project necessitates.

"The idea process is the toughest part of what I do," Erik said. "I subject my ideas to a four-point test before I even begin to think, 'Okay, this is a plausible thing.' That's why it takes me at least a year between the time I've finished a book and the start of the next project. First of all, it has to be interesting to me. It's got to be something I'm willing to live with for three, four, or five years. It has to have a built-in natural narrative arc.

"Nothing can be artificial. In the case of the *Lusitania* [the subject of Erik's book *Dead Wake*], it's ship sets out, ship sinks. That's the arc. You know where it's going. You just have to get there in a suspenseful, articulate way. Then there has to be—and this is nonnegotiable—a very rich, detailed archival base of material for that particular story. It can't just be that you're drawing on secondary sources. You must have access to the real deal so that you get texture, quotes, and things that other people may have overlooked or ignored.

"Once you hit all those bases, then it's time to do a book proposal, which is what I always do. Even though my agent says, 'You can just write me a letter at this point,' I always say, 'No, no.' I'm so glad because you can get yourself into real trouble just sending a letter to your agent or to an editor to say, 'This is what I plan to do, it's a no-brainer, this is going to work.' I always do a very detailed proposal, which consists of an initial sample chapter, an essay on the nature of the subject, how I'm going to write it, what the narrative arc is, what the sources are, the whole deal. Then a capsule outline with chapter summaries that give a gist of how the story will progress.

"After I've gone through that exercise—which is as much for me as anybody—if I'm still interested and still think that this is a go, that's very helpful. I've killed some projects when I have finished the book proposal and thought to myself, 'There's something missing. It just lacks heart.' At that point when I'm done with the proposal and if I'm still going to do the project, I'm pretty confident that it's going to work for me and that it's also going to work for a publisher."

⚡ **CREATIVE SPARKS 2** ⚡

List your top five creative ideas, then rate them on interest, impact, and resources. Commit to the highest-rated one, like a book idea that aligns with your passion and available research, and start developing it into a lasting work of art.

HARNESSING SELF-DOUBT AS CREATIVE FUEL

One might assume that a creator who has "made it" has their emotional world perfectly in order. However, even masterful musicians, actors, and writers like Erik grapple with the same internal challenges as everyone else. They must overcome their lack of self-confidence, recognize when their thoughts distort reality, and silence the negative self-talk that plays in their heads. This is especially crucial when tackling ambitious projects that can take years to complete.

"I have a tendency toward self-doubt and, in a way, it's not a bad thing because it powers you to do whatever it takes to overcome what's causing that," Erik said. "I'll give you a very specific example. My book *The Splendid and the Vile* is about Churchill, the Blitz period, his family, and advisers. When I was first setting out on this topic, I was pretty confident that I had a good fresh window that it was going to be something new and different in a realm that is obviously crowded."

However, a conversation with his daughter, who is also a writer, made him wonder if he had anything original to say on a subject that already had many books written about it. "She asked me at one of our lunches what I was working on. And so, two glasses of wine in, I told her. She looked at me and said, 'You actually look troubled. Dad; what could you possibly say that's new?' That kept running through my head while I was working on the book. But again, there's a positive side to this because it drives you to say something new, to do the research that uncovers the thing that makes it fresh. So it wasn't entirely a negative thing," he said.

"But this is one reason why I almost never tell people what I'm working on other than my wife and a few close friends, because the reactions they have can really infuse that self-talk. One time I was at a family reunion and my older sister was badgering me about the book I was working on at that time. I said, 'I'm not going to tell you.' She kept at it, so finally I said, 'Okay.' This was for my book *Thunderstruck* about [Guglielmo] Marconi and [Harvey Hawley] Crippen. I described the book and what it was, and she said, 'Oh, I wouldn't read that.' And that went through my head for ever and ever."

Unlike a novelist who has to create an entire story from scratch, a narrative nonfiction author obtains source materials from letters, newspapers, diaries, and other historical sources. Some might see this as a tiresome process, but for authors like Erik, part of the joy in book writing is sifting through seemingly endless archive collections to find the kind of telling details that put his readers in the story. He prefers this to online research, which hampers his sense of discovery. This is why, after he had read a couple of books about Churchill, he started searching for original ideas to write his own.

"I plunged into the archives because that's where I feel comfortable and that's where I know I am going to find new material," Erik said. "I just know it, mainly because with my books I'm trying to open a new window on something and not just do the same old, same old. It's a strange phenomenon: I don't know what I'm looking for, but I will know it when I find it. That's what makes the whole archival thing fun. Every day is a potential discovery for something that's going to make the book.

"You never waste time in an archive. If you go venturing in and you're getting stuff, and you find things that just are completely useless, it's never a loss because it goes into the mix. It's there, somewhere in your brain. And because you're venturing in along a different path, it could be something brand new that nobody else has found before.

"I'm still a big believer in the idea of throwing that net wide and looking at things. Anybody who is really focused will say, 'That's not going to be productive.' But so often that's where the best stuff resides."

⚡ CREATIVE SPARKS 3 ⚡

Think of a time when self-doubt crept in during a project. Remind yourself that these feelings are normal and don't define your abilities or success. Your doubts may stem from your passion and deep investment in the work. Acknowledge that you've prepared well, and that self-doubt is part of the journey. The next time doubt arises, recognize it, but stay grounded in your preparation and passion.

STAYING PATIENT AND PERSISTENT

One of the things Erik learned during his experiences at the *Bucks County Courier Times* and *The Wall Street Journal* was the importance of planning and persistence over speed. Despite not being the fastest writer, his self-awareness and methodical approach have served him well.

"I was never actually very good at deadlines," Erik said. "I always met them, but I was not like some of these cold-blooded rewrite guys or writers who thrive on the deadline thing, nail it, and can do a whole-column *Wall Street Journal* leader in a day, starting with the reporting in the morning and finishing it that night. That's not me—I can't do that."

In terms of book deadlines, Erik emphasized the importance of a gradual approach. "You can't rush. It's like erosion. You have to do it bit by bit by bit. If you leave it too close to the point when you're going to turn that book in, (a) you're going to hate yourself, and (b) you're going to miss that deadline because books do not lend themselves to the all-nighter approach to writing. I never even pulled an all-nighter in college. I was always systematic about studying. I always meet my deadlines because I anticipate them way in advance."

Knowing that he prefers to slowly chip away at his desired word count, Erik maintains a persistent writing method that keeps his momentum going throughout each project. He utilizes a two-phase approach: doing most of the research and then writing the book.

"My daily routine varies depending on the phase," Erik explained. "This first one I refer to as the 'page-a-day phase.' I get up early, 4:30 or 5:00 AM. I'll do one page and generally get that done by 7:00 in the morning. After that one page, the important thing is that I stop. Maybe it will be a page and a half, maybe it'll be a page and a paragraph, whatever. But the important thing that I've learned from experience is to always stop at a place where I know I can pick up. Stop in the middle of a sentence, stop in the middle of a paragraph. And I do that religiously because the worst thing you can do as a writer, I think, is binge-write.

"I do that page a day seven days a week when I'm in that phase. I'm a big believer in the idea that inspiration is much overrated. You've got to be at your desk for it to arrive. I often tell writing students on those rare occasions when I teach that if you're waiting for a bus, it helps to be at the bus stop," Erik said.

His page-a-day mode lasts for about three months. As he gathers momentum, this then becomes two and four pages a day. But even as he gets into the full flow of his manuscript, Eric avoids binge writing, stepping away from his keyboard around noon to focus on other aspects of the process.

"The page-a-day mode will probably go on for about three months. In the afternoon I'm researching. And then a page a day becomes—just by the sheer nature of the beast—two pages a day, then four. And then the next thing you know, it's full-blown writing to get the book done. But even then, I do not binge. I stop at around noon, and then I'll continue doing research in the afternoon or rewriting, editing, or cutting and pasting. That's a big part of the process for me."

In between his morning writing and afternoon editing, researching, and cutting and pasting, Erik is deliberate in making time for hobbies that have nothing to do with his profession. Chief among these are cooking and playing tennis with friends in New York, where he moved from Seattle in 2019.

"Tennis is a big part of my life in terms of just pulling me out of the angst of researching and writing because you can't think about what you're working on when you're playing. On those days when I play tennis, I generally take somewhere around 23,000 steps and 25 flights of stairs.

And that makes me feel very satisfied. You've got to stay healthy when you're writing. You have to retain your perspective and keep the writing under control."

⚡ CREATIVE SPARKS 4 ⚡

Consistent effort often outweighs quick results in any endeavor. How can you establish a sustainable routine that includes dedicated work time and rejuvenating breaks? Balancing work and relaxation will keep your creativity thriving.

MASTERING THE ART OF REVISION

While the process of writing a book is much longer than composing a feature story, there is some crossover, and Erik still calls on experiences from his reporter days to enhance his initial manuscript drafts. After turning in his first long article for *The Wall Street Journal*, his bureau chief cut it up into pieces, reassembled it with tape, and handed it back like he was unfurling a scroll.

"I went through it and realized that he really helped find the structure," Erik said. "Forever afterward, I have used that method for everything that I've written that's over two pages. I think it's just about foolproof.

"I guarantee you will find places where the material duplicates, where you realize that two things have to be next to each other that were separated by four or five paragraphs. I've applied that over time also to books, where in the end phase I will lay out the entire book on the floor and move things around, cutting, pasting, just to see what the natural structure is. That's been invaluable to me."

Once Erik has laid out the scraps of his story and rearranged them like a giant literary jigsaw puzzle, it's time to subject his work to even sterner scrutiny. He realized a long time ago that each manuscript must not only look right before he submits it to his publisher but also read and sound right. Erik believes that these extra layers of quality control improve the final product.

"When I've got a complete first draft, I always read it aloud," he said. "Maybe not contiguously from page one to page four hundred, but at some point, I will have read every single word. When I'm doing that, I often find it very helpful to play a soundtrack that matches the nature of the material. For example, I found for one of my books—I think it was *Isaac's Storm*—the soundtrack to *Titanic* was very effective. The soundtrack that was really terrific when I was working on *The Devil in the White City* was George Winston's album *Plains*. The music went perfectly with the book."

While Erik is reading his work to himself aloud and making the necessary cuts and corrections, he also calls in outside help to further refine his story and ensure that his narrative arc is on track.

"My wife is very involved in the process," Erik said. "When I finally have a working draft, she's a terrific help because she is what I think of as my ideal reader. She represents the audience that I am trying to reach. Someone who may not necessarily have a whole lot of knowledge about whatever the subject is or much interest in it but is going to sink into that past era and come out thinking, 'Wow, that was an interesting experience. That was fascinating.'"

Erik's wife is a natural editor, and he describes her as his "secret weapon" who points out things that he should cut, keep, or expand upon.

"Her primary symbols are a smiley face, a crying face, and a little sad face but with two streams of tears dotting from the eyes," he said. "Also, an up arrow, which I know from experience means something is good. We keep that no matter what. A down arrow means cut it. The most troubling is this long series of receding Zzzs, which means that she was bored. When I see those, I realize I've got to do something—either cut or trim. She'll also add some notes to clarify something. The reason we established this practice is because having somebody else read your stuff can be a conflict-filled moment. We've worked out a system where it removes all of that. It's very effective."

⚡ **CREATIVE SPARKS 5** ⚡

Having a structured revision process is crucial. How can you implement a "cut-up and rearrange" method or include someone else's perspective to enhance your work's flow and organization? Experiment with this technique to see how it can improve the clarity and impact of your writing.

PURSUING RELENTLESS EXCELLENCE

Though he welcomes his early readers' feedback, Erik has found that once a book is published, he has to insulate himself from good and bad reviews to preserve his peace of mind.

"I have never been particularly good at taking criticism," Erik said. "When you've finished the book, you're done with it. You're not going to go back and rewrite it to respond to somebody's critique. I suppose in an ideal world, somebody's review of your book will help you write the next one. It doesn't work that way for me because my books are very different each time around.

"Before the book comes out, I'm great with criticism. If people want to critique my narrative before I get into the final draft, I'm okay with that. For my recent book [*The Splendid and the Vile*], I hired a professional fact-checker, and she was great. It's the first time I've ever done that, and I will do it forever after. I also sent the manuscript out to three Churchill experts for them to read and to weigh in and that was incredibly valuable.

"But after publication, I try to avoid reading reviews. As it happens, you can't really because people will tell you things. Especially now in the age of Twitter, your fans will say, 'Oh, that reviewer didn't know what the hell he was talking about.' And I'm like, 'What reviewer? What review?' I scrupulously avoid this stuff because if it's a bad review, it's going to piss me off and it's going to be rattling around in my brain forever. Even if it's a really good review, I'll find something that will annoy me. So it's best that reviews and I keep our distance. The thing I can't stand is when a reviewer flogs a personal ideology or when an entity hires someone to do the review who is clearly a competitor. That drives me nuts."

Many writers would be satisfied with seven *New York Times* best-sellers, over nine million copies sold worldwide, and having one of their books turned into a TV series (Martin Scorsese and Leonardo DiCaprio are set to produce a series based on *The Devil in the White City* for Hulu). Not Erik. For him, the joy isn't in the royalty checks or critical acclaim but rather in the process of researching, interviewing, writing, and editing that has become his life's work.

"What drives me, what keeps me going with books is that there's always [the question of] what that next idea is going to be. And the fascination, the challenge of turning that into the next book. I love it and I don't think I'll ever stop. My intention is to drop dead at my desk."

For Erik, the journey of crafting each book is where his passion truly lies. His relentless pursuit of excellence is a testament to his dedication to the art of storytelling.

✎ CREATIVE SPARKS 6 ✎

Decide when feedback is helpful versus harmful, and consider what type of input you need at each stage—big-picture ideas early on, or detailed critiques later. Establish a system that invites constructive criticism while protecting your creative vision, allowing you to refine and excel in your work.

THE 5 Cs IN ERIK LARSON'S JOURNEY

Erik Larson's journey from a curious journalist to a bestselling author exemplifies the principles of mental toughness through the 5 Cs:

1. **Courage:** Erik displayed immense courage by leaving a stable job at *The Wall Street Journal* to pursue a less predictable career in book writing. Despite early setbacks, his bold decisions underlined his readiness to embrace uncertainty, paving the way for his later success.

2. **Confidence:** Erik consistently believed in his storytelling abilities, even amid doubts and external skepticism. His commitment to thorough research and crafting compelling narratives reinforced his confidence, enabling him to author bestsellers.

3. **Concentration:** Erik's disciplined writing strategy—focusing on one page a day and stopping at a juncture conducive to continuation—demonstrates his deep concentration. This method helps him stay immersed and maintain steady progress in his work.

4. **Composure:** Facing deadlines and potential doubts, Erik keeps his composure by integrating activities like tennis and cooking into his routine. This balanced approach ensures he remains calm and focused, channeling his energies productively into his writing.

5. **Commitment:** Erik's dedication to his writing is shown through rigorous research, meticulous editing, and a commitment to continuous improvement. His persistent efforts, even when confronted with challenges, underscore his dedication to delivering quality storytelling.

YOUR CREATIVE TOOLKIT

Just as Erik Larson exemplifies the 5 Cs of mental toughness in his journey as a bestselling author, celebrated for his compelling storytelling and meticulous re-creation of the past, you, too, can develop these strengths. Here are practical tips and tools based on the 5 Cs of creativity inspired by his journey.

1. **Courage:**
   - **Challenge Yourself with Affirmations:** Boost your confidence before tackling creative challenges by repeating positive affirmations like "I am brave and capable" or "I trust myself to handle new challenges." For instance, a painter might use these affirmations to build confidence when accepting a commission in an artistic style they've never attempted before.
   - **Reframe Discomfort as Growth:** Embrace discomfort as a sign of progress and boundary-pushing. Recognize that feeling uneasy means you're growing and developing as a person and artist. For example, a writer attending a public reading of their work for the first time can view their nerves as an indicator of personal and professional growth.
   - **Take Bold Leaps:** Step outside your comfort zone and take bold actions, even if they come with risks. Each courageous step strengthens your resilience and fuels your creative passion. A musician might showcase an original song at an open mic night, embracing the fear of judgment as a catalyst for growth.

2. **Confidence:**
   - **Envision Excellence:** Vividly imagine your next achievement, engaging all senses. See the triumph, hear the accolades, and feel the pride. Regular visualization builds confidence and readiness. Make it a habit to mentally rehearse success.
   - **Cultivate Balanced Self-Talk:** Acknowledge strengths and successes without exaggeration, while addressing weaknesses with constructive self-reflection. Example: "I excelled due to hard work and skill, but I can improve my technique further."
   - **Celebrate Daily Wins:** Create "trophy moments" by tackling challenging tasks, then briefly imagine standing on a podium, basking in pride. Celebrate small victories to build momentum and reinforce confidence.

3. **Concentration:**
   - **World-Hop with Intention:** Imagine slipping into a magical realm when you enter your creative zone. As you transition from art to life, visualize stepping out of that world and into another. This mental switch helps you fully immerse in your craft, then seamlessly shift gears to tackle other tasks. Think of it like a painter donning a studio cloak, or a writer stepping into a fictional world!
   - **Role-Play with Abandon:** Dive headfirst into each creative role, embracing the character, craft, or canvas. Let go of distractions and fully embody the part—like an actor becoming one with their character. When the scene ends, take off the costume and step into the next role with equal enthusiasm!
   - **Mind-Surf with Ease:** As you shift between creative worlds, catch any stray thoughts or concerns and jot them down. This mental bookmarking helps you stay present and focused, ensuring a smooth transition. Imagine a musician scribbling down song ideas before riding the wave to the next task—no mental ripples or distractions!

4. **Composure:**
   - **Fuel Your Fire:** Ignite your creativity. Channel frustration from work and life into art, music, or writing. Repeat: "I transform anger into artistic expression." And watch your passion ignite!
   - **Breathe, Reflect, Create:** Mindfully manage anger's spark. Breathe deep, meditate, or talk it out. Then create with intention. Remember: "I breathe in calm, and create with purpose." And find peace in the process!
   - **Set Boundaries, Unleash Growth:** Establish creative boundaries to tame anger's triggers. Communicate your needs clearly and seek support. Empower yourself with: "I set boundaries, transform anger, and thrive." And celebrate your freedom!

5. **Commitment:**
   - **Dream Big, Decide Bigger:** Imagine two versions of yourself: the "Rockstar You" and the "What-If You." Use this contrast to fuel your daily choices. Picture your future self crushing it in your creative field—and let that motivate you to put in the work!
   - **Choose Your Masterpiece:** Every decision is a brushstroke on the canvas of your life. Choose to paint a masterpiece of fulfillment! Spend time on your passion, and watch your dreams take shape. Remember, every hour devoted to your craft brings you closer to the "Rockstar You"!
   - **Align Your Path:** At every crossroads, pause and ask: "Does this choice harmonize with my creative vision?" Make decisions that resonate with your long-term goals. Celebrate each aligned choice with a triumphant affirmation: "I'm crafting my dream reality, one decision at a time!"

IN THE FINAL CHAPTER

Join Chris Burkard on a journey where stunning adventure photography meets passionate environmental advocacy. His awe-inspiring images showcase the untamed beauty of remote landscapes while highlighting their vulnerability. We'll look at how his love for exploration and sense of purpose drive his creative vision.

Chapter 12

PICTURE THIS: CHRIS BURKARD

*S*now *whips around the rugged white Land Rover Defender as an Arctic wind hurls flakes faster and harder across the unbroken Icelandic tundra. Inside, the photographer, filmmaker, and surfers huddle deep in their down jackets, braving the worst winter storm in a quarter century. Despite near-zero visibility and blizzard conditions, the crew pushes their vehicle slowly forward, determined to capture the Northern Lights, showcasing their resilience and commitment.*

This scene of resilience and determination mirrors the life of Chris Burkard, a photographer from Arroyo Grande, California, just a stone's throw from the famous surf haven of Pismo Beach. His formative years were filled with sand, waves, and a passion for surfing, bodysurfing, and boogie boarding. As much as he loved participating in water sports, Chris also began playing the role of chronicler, photographing his fellow surfers as they pinged out of barrels by the pier or dropped into a beach break wave. When they eventually came back onto dry land, the budding entrepreneur tried to sell them their action shots.

After graduating high school, Chris enrolled at nearby Cuesta Junior

College. Like a surfer stuck in an undertow, he'd already felt the irresistible pull of photography, but it was still a curiosity rather than a calling. However, as he delved into courses on black-and-white photography and other subjects, the seed planted in Pismo Beach began to sprout. Chris realized traditional education couldn't fulfill his aspirations, leading him to tell his parents he was leaving school to pursue a career as a surf photographer.

FACING THE UNKNOWN

Chris faced a significant challenge when transitioning to a full-time career in photography. "Fear propelled my decision," he said. "It was the fear of falling into the same job I watched my dad do." This feeling pushed him to a pivotal moment, where he had to choose between predictability and stepping out into the unknown.

He understood that opportunities do not wait for anyone. "Sometimes you're at this train station, bags half-packed, and an opportunity speeds by. To seize it, you must board the train before you're fully ready."

Chris faced hurdles, including resistance from his parents, when he chose photography over academics. "I had straight As, scholarships, and I was set to be the only person to go to college in my family. It felt like I was going to let them down and that was really challenging." Chris recalled.

Despite intense pressure, Chris recognized the necessity of forging his own unpredictable path and embracing the unknown. "I had this fear of ending up stuck in the status quo, on a path where I knew the outcome and exactly where it was going to end," Chris said. "I felt like I needed something in my life that was going to give me a little more uncertainty, that was going to provide me with the opportunity to rise to the occasion.

"What occasion that was, I didn't know. Because although I dreamt of being a surf photographer, I was also very realistic about the fact that I would have shot anything to make a living as a photographer."

↗ **CREATIVE SPARKS 1** ↗

Chris's journey underscores the importance of taking bold risks. Have you ever felt a strong urge to pursue a different path? Identify your creative direction and embrace the fear of venturing beyond familiar territory, even if it means challenging the status quo.

PUSHING LIMITS FOR THE PERFECT SHOT

This isn't the part of the story where Chris becomes an overnight success, suddenly picking and choosing prime assignments worldwide. It didn't happen that way. Like many creatives, Chris endured hardships and paid his dues before landing clients like Apple, Montblanc, and Lufthansa.

"I lived below the poverty level," Chris recalled. "I scraped pennies off the floor of my Toyota Tacoma, using every spare cent to buy gas and drive up and down the California coast to shoot photographs. You're chasing the eternal sunrise, eternal sunshine, and good waves. And that didn't leave much room for health or income or anything. I was just trying to create as much as I could. So everything was going into traveling and staying busy doing that, which was really hard. It was a crazy scenario."

Despite the hardships, Chris's dedication eventually paid off. In 2006, he applied for an internship at *Transworld Surfer* magazine and, to his surprise, got the gig. A few months later, he was promoted to assistant photo editor. He also spent time shadowing Michael Fatali, a landscape photographer famed for his stunning shots of desert scenes in the American Southwest.

Chris quickly made his mark and accepted the senior staff photographer position at Surfline while also working for *Water Magazine*. Then, in 2010, the iconic *Surfer* magazine offered him a job, prompting another move. As he advanced in magazine photojournalism, he dipped his toes in the publishing world.

Around the same time, Chris was awarded the inaugural Follow the Light Foundation grant, established in memory of legendary surf photographer Larry Moore. This grant enabled Chris to embark on a six-month odyssey along the Pacific coastline. He and collaborator Eric Soderquist surfed all day at various spots, joined strangers for meals around campfires at night, and then drove their old creaky VW van to the next beach or break the following morning. The result was a sumptuously photographed coffee table book, *The California Surf Project*.

This trip sparked a love of adventuring that quickly burst into flame. While he enjoyed certain elements of working for water sports magazines, Chris soon realized that a career as a staff photographer or contributing editor wasn't for him; he wanted the creative freedom to roam wherever his curiosity took him. Sticking to surf photography was the easier path, but Chris refused to be pigeonholed for the rest of his career. So he went back to square one, digging deep and putting in years of hard work to establish credibility on commercial shoots and ambitious passion projects that took him worldwide.

"Hustle has been critical to everything that I do," Chris said. "I'm still hustling now. The beauty of it is that I've forgone retainers and the opportunity to have a consistent income because I wanted to experience what it fully feels like to be present in the work I'm doing. I look forward to opportunities where I can give a piece of myself and be constantly challenged. Five years ago, I could've sat back on my laurels and been like, 'It's never going to get any better than this.' But somebody younger, smarter, and harder is going to come along, so I feel like I have to hustle now more than ever."

Chris's relentless drive and dedication to his craft are evident. "If you take this mentality into the job, you're never going to get bored or disinterested. Forcing myself to appreciate what is ultimately mine for the taking is to me what keeps me going. That's what keeps me inspired. If in five years I have to reinvent myself yet still have my creativity to fall back on, I don't mind that. I've done that multiple times because my career started as a photographer and elevated to directing and VPing films, and then to working as a storyteller with books. I'm constantly looking to reinvent myself, and I feel like those who get left in the dust are the ones who don't."

The photography-loving public often only sees the final output of a process that might take Chris days, weeks, or even months to complete. They don't understand the days spent in freezing water and on top of windswept peaks, or the effort required to scope out, select, and reach the perfect spots for that one elusive shot—let alone the thousands of hours of storyboarding, filming, and editing that it takes to finish a film like Chris's *Unnur*, which was an official selection at the Lighthouse International Film Festival.

"I pulled out my hair because of stress—literally, chunks of my hair," Chris said. "I have pterygiums in both eyes and bad hearing because my ears are closed off from bone overgrowth from swimming in cold water. I've had varicose vein surgery. I don't really want to give a full list of that stuff because it's a shitty way of looking at it. The reality is that all of it is elective suffering, and those wounds, scars, and things that I deal with now are just reminders of a life well lived, and stories that I embedded deep within myself. Yeah, of course, they affect my day-to-day—my sleep and mood—but ultimately, I feel stronger because of them."

When asked about his big break, Chris was candid. "At a certain point when someone is asking me for advice, the next question is inevitably, 'What was your big break?' There wasn't one. I joke that I'm an overnight success that took fourteen years. I don't know any route other than the long and hard one because that's the path I chose. Nothing was ever given to me, and everything was earned. Because of this, I've always felt gratitude for what it has provided me: the experiences, the opportunities, every time I come home to my family. There's food on the table and money in the bank because of the work that I've put in."

Chris told us about the importance of having a deeper motivation beyond material rewards. "You're going to need a driving force at some point. Something better than collecting a paycheck and stamps in your passport," he said. "When I was very young, that was the driving force, that's what I cared about. But I realized very quickly that it wasn't enough. You need to seek out something bigger, like providing for your family, sharing stories, and hopefully changing people's lives in some way. That comes back to your mission statement. I'm not saying that it always has to be an altruistic goal, but the hope is that the more altruistic or the more meaningful it is, the more willing you're going to be to do it long term."

✎ CREATIVE SPARKS 2 ✎

Picture a video of you fully committed, both feet in, grinding away at your creative dreams. What do others see? What do you want them to see? What drives you to conquer obstacles and keep creating? Craft a long-term vision that surpasses monetary rewards, fueling your passion indefinitely.

SELECTIVE SACRIFICE

Beyond the physical ramifications of venturing into harsh and unforgiving terrains, Chris's relentless quest to hone his craft has come at a significant cost in other ways. Although he can now assess and select his projects more carefully, it wasn't always that way as he sought to build up his business and bolster his portfolio.

"In the last few years, I've had to sacrifice less," Chris said. "That's the goal, right? If you're fifteen years into a career and you're sacrificing more than you have in the beginning, there's something wrong and you probably should pack it in. But the way I like to look at my career or any creative endeavor is the fact that it's all about the parable of the four burners.

"Imagine a stove with four burners. One represents health, another business, the third relationships, and the fourth family. At the beginning of my career, I turned the health and relationships burners way, way down. As the saying goes, 'If you want to be successful, you have to turn down one burner. If you want to be really successful, you have to turn down two.'"

Reflecting on his early career, Chris acknowledged the toll it took on his well-being and social connections. "My college experience was thwarted by the fact that I wanted a career. And my health was definitely not a priority, though it is now. I've never felt so sick and depleted than when those sleepless nights turned into sleepless months and then sleepless years early in my career."

He also sacrificed many personal relationships in pursuit of his goals. "I've had a lot of my relationships suffer—friends that I didn't know anymore and people that I wasn't willing to talk to because I poured everything into my career. So I would say that to me, it was all about business and family. That's a really challenging thing to acknowledge, let alone talk about, because I know full well that these were burners that I purposefully turned down. It's taken the last couple of years to try and slowly turn them back on."

As a creator, you will inevitably question your abilities or feel overwhelmed by a project's complexities. This is when confidence is crucial. Remember, the skills that brought you here will help you succeed in challenging circumstances. Even the most accomplished artists face self-doubt and must push through to do their best work.

"Every day I pick up a camera, I feel imposter syndrome because I'm still blown away that this is my career," Chris admitted. "But the reality is that you don't just jump into those situations. I slowly but surely gained an appreciation of where I was at in my skill set and when I took an assignment and put myself out there, I had already worked hard building a portfolio that was competent."

He stressed the importance of preparation and self-investment. "If you're not investing time and money into generating portfolios that you feel comfortable about and safe in sharing, then you need to question why you're doing it. If I wanted to shoot an automotive campaign, I wouldn't wait for somebody to hire me because they felt in their heart of hearts that I'd be good for it. I would spend my time going out shooting cars, so by the time I was ready to be hired for a job like that, I felt ready."

Chris acknowledged that the feeling of being an imposter might persist, but preparation can mitigate it. "You're still going to feel like an imposter when you're doing it but at least you'll be wearing the right clothes, using the right lingo, and asking the right questions. If pushing the trigger buttons feels foreign in some way, that's a feeling that will go away with time, but you can't fake all the other things."

Understanding that feelings of imposter syndrome are common can be reassuring. These feelings often reflect admirable qualities such as a commitment to excellence, a drive to learn, and a healthy dose of humility. Embrace a learning mindset while staying confident in your abilities. This balance helps you avoid complacency and maintain a grounded perspective. Self-acceptance means recognizing that who you are today is okay.

✔ CREATIVE SPARKS 3 ✔

What sacrifices are you willing to make for your creative ambitions? How can you maintain a balance between your well-being, relationships, and creative passion? Reflect on Chris's "four burners" metaphor—health, business, relationships, and family—and find ways to give all areas of your life the attention they need.

MAINTAINING SELF-WORTH AND RESILIENCE

In the age of social media, a creator's self-worth can easily become tied to followers and post engagement. For authors and musicians, this extends to royalty checks and bestseller lists; for filmmakers, it's box office numbers. Reviews from critics and fans also provide either positive reinforcement or discouragement.

Even for an award-winning photographer and filmmaker like Chris, the constant push and pull between intrinsic and extrinsic factors can impact his psyche. "If there's a single greatest challenge in my career—and I'll be as bold to say any creative person's career—it's dealing with self-worth," Chris said. "Nowadays, we seek self-worth in social media. And it's a very dangerous game because by doing that you're constantly trying to better yourself. You're always trying to have a deeper, more engaging this or that."

"All of my self-worth used to be derived from the idea that I could pay," Chris said. "I could put food on the table. I could buy a new pair of wheels so there wasn't metal showing through my tires. Self-worth came from the fact that somebody was willing to give me an income to do this job. To make ends meet. And that was the most humbling thing that I feel like I've ever experienced. To this day, I take great pride in the fact that I get to call this a career, and it allows me to support not only myself but also my family and employees."

While Chris's art, shared with over four million followers, may appear serene, the conditions he endures to create it are often chaotic and grueling. Take the winter surfing trip to Iceland that Chris captured in his acclaimed documentary *Under an Arctic Sky*, when a blizzard threatened to derail the entire shoot. Facing such adversity requires a creator not only to develop fortitude and grit but also to recharge in between demanding projects.

"When I'm home I try to cultivate a deep well of inspiration," Chris said. "I try to spend my time doing the things that inspire me with people that inspire me. Because when I'm out on a shoot away from my family, I'm waking up in the middle of the night and it's so cold that I don't want to get out of my tent, I have to remind myself if I wanted to stay warm and stay comfortable, I should have just stayed home."

Chris emphasized the importance of embracing hardship to fuel his creative drive. "I'm there to feel discomfort. I fill up my well with inspiration so that when I'm on assignment I can dip into it. That means giving time to my health, riding my bike, doing yoga, going surfing, spending time with my kids, and taking time to meditate. I'm preparing myself before going out on a shoot. That way when I get there, I'm good for ten or fifteen days in a never-ending, no-sleep situation. I've already prepared for it."

During assignments, Chris adeptly adjusts to the lack of his typical grounding routines, maintaining his resilience and focus. "On an assignment, I'm in a situation where there isn't time to do my morning routine, eat the food I want to eat, or call my wife. All the things that normally ground me aren't available. It comes down to giving everything to the places that I love."

He draws inspiration from his surroundings and the people he works with. "When I'm shooting work that I feel satisfied by, I can pull inspiration from a landscape or the people I'm with. It acts as fuel. There's something to be said for being in places where I feel motivated. For me, that might be Yosemite or Iceland, where I've been forty-one times. I feel like I can draw from places like that."

⚡ CREATIVE SPARKS 4 ⚡

How can you measure your self-worth beyond external validation? Identify activities or places that "fill your well" and sustain your creativity during tough projects. Establish a routine to recharge and maintain your resilience.

PURSUING THE 10,000-HOUR RULE

In the book *Outliers,* Malcolm Gladwell introduced the "10,000-hour rule" to the mainstream. It has become a convenient way to summarize the lengthy process needed to go from beginner to master. Gladwell based this on the work of Anders Ericsson, who spent his career studying how violinists, pianists, and other creators and high performers became experts. He suggested that engaging in deliberate practice—which is goal-oriented, purposeful, and focused on tasks just beyond your current skill level—is essential.

In Chris's case, his expertise in photography, filmmaking, and storytelling was forged by thousands of miles, hundreds of early mornings, and countless hours of editing. Now he's able to get and stay in the zone more readily by picking and choosing his spots.

"You work and work and shoot your first 10,000 photographs, and then the camera becomes a part of you," Chris said. "The creative process becomes easier because you're not held up by the technical side. Now I can pull a camera out and know exactly what to do. That's a freeing feeling. That's the spot I aim to be in, working in a familiar landscape and medium, picturing the photograph I want and manifesting it. The experience unfolds, and I'm just getting myself in the right position."

Chris believes that his improvement is largely because of how practice has taught him when to pick exactly the right times to take pictures. "I am in no way a great technical photographer, but I shoot much fewer images than I ever have before," he said. "In the beginning of my career, I just sprayed and prayed, hoping for a good result. The difference now isn't that I can shoot a better image, but that I've learned to recognize when moments are truly special and to document the hell out of them. I'm dedicating my time and space more to where it counts."

As a creator, it can be tempting to be a generalist. That's what is taught in school, and there's a huge body of work in the blogosphere, podcasting, and creative corners of bookstores filled with the message that you have to do everything well rather than specialize. While he keeps expanding his range, Chris is also self-aware enough to know where his strengths lie and continues to rigorously develop these skills.

"I came into photography with the mindset of 'I have to do everything,'" Chris said. "At a certain point, I realized that when I was putting my portfolio in front of an editor, this wasn't what they were looking for. They don't want somebody that can shoot weddings and portraits. They're usually looking to hire somebody because they're the best at what they do. That made me determined to hone my knife set and make sure I've got a couple of really sharp knives. I have some dull ones, too, but those aren't the ones I'm going to pull out in a knife fight."

Chris gave the example of another specialist to underline his point: "Paul Nicklen is hired to shoot under Arctic ice because he's the best at it in the world. Can he shoot Afghan portraiture? Yeah. But does he get assignments to do that? No. There's a reality that he has embraced, and I've tried to do the same with the things I'm good at. Yes, I am still actively participating in growing, learning, and doing a better job at other things, but I'm not letting that hold me back from strengthening my core set of skills. It's a healthy place when you know what you're best at and can work from there."

⚡ **CREATIVE SPARKS 5** ⚡

True expertise is achieved through deliberate practice, not short-cuts. How can you push your creative boundaries and enhance your core skills to distinguish yourself? Commit to continuous learning within your niche for a more effortless creative flow.

CHARTING YOUR CREATIVE PATH

When people see Chris's finished work—whether it's a movie, a commercial, or a photograph on his Instagram feed—they see high quality. However, like every creator, Chris experiences both peaks and slumps. Many of his images end up on the cutting room floor or deleted from his cameras' SD cards.

"I deal with slumps all the time. There are moments when it's hard for me to stay motivated or excited about a project," Chris shared. "When that happens, I ask myself, 'Why am I doing this in the first place?' The COVID-19 pandemic reminded me of the importance of seizing the moment. Nothing lasts forever, and we aren't immune to life's challenges."

To combat creative slumps, Chris taps into a well of inspiration. "If 99.9 percent of my life was occupied by photography, I'd burn out 100 percent. So I find other ways to exercise my creative freedom. It's about constantly moving forward. Stagnation is the death of any creative pursuit. Constant growth is essential—seeking opportunities in other areas helps me work through stagnation and opens up new spaces. When I revisit that stuck point later, I have new perspectives."

Saying no to projects that don't align with his goals has been crucial for Chris. "You can learn to say no so that you're really saying yes to what you want," Chris said, referencing Greg McKeown's book *Essentialism*. "I used to say yes to everything because that's what I saw my dad do. But now I'm more selective about the projects I choose, focusing on what truly matters."

Chris has developed a set of filters to evaluate potential projects, allowing him to focus his energy on endeavors that align with his values. This strategic approach has enabled Burkard Studios to thrive, helping Chris achieve a harmonious balance between work, family, friendships, and health. "A project has to fit certain criteria. Does it make me happy? Will it fulfill me? Will it support my business? Is it healthy for the environment or allow me to advocate for something? I'm looking for collaborators that fit within my ethos," he said.

Defining a mission statement has been crucial for Chris. He advises every creator to ask themselves, "What are you trying to accomplish? What are you trying to say? The clearer you get on that, the better you understand your aspirations. When people ask for advice, I tell them, 'If you don't have a destination in mind, it's hard to draw your roadmap.'"

Reflecting on his journey, Chris spoke about the importance of passion. "Making a decision based on your hopes and dreams rather than the safe route is challenging and tests you in every capacity. But that's the goal. If you're not willing to suffer for what you love, then you don't have a passion for it. Passion literally means suffering. Ask yourself, 'What am I willing to suffer for?' That's the easiest way to figure out what you should be doing."

Chris's journey underscores essential principles for any creator. Asking fundamental questions about motivation can reignite passion, and saying no to misaligned opportunities helps focus energy. Growth comes from pushing through lows and celebrating highs. Align projects with your values, stay open to new inspirations, and keep your goals in sight.

⚡ CREATIVE SPARKS 6 ⚡

How can you revive your passion during creative slumps? Think about diversifying your outlets, aligning your projects with your values, and defining a clear mission statement. Passion often requires sacrifice—what are you willing to "suffer for" to reach your creative objectives?

THE 5 Cs IN CHRIS BURKARD'S JOURNEY

Chris Burkard's journey from a California surf kid to a world-renowned adventure photographer exemplifies the principles of mental toughness through the 5 Cs:

1. **Courage:** Chris demonstrated immense courage when he decided to leave traditional education and pursue a career in surf photography. Facing the unknown, he followed his passion despite the fear of falling into a conventional job. This leap of faith propelled him into a challenging but fulfilling career.

2. **Confidence:** Building a portfolio that showcased his skills, Chris overcame feelings of imposter syndrome by preparing thoroughly for every opportunity. His dedication to mastering his craft, even in harsh conditions, boosted his confidence and established him as a respected photographer.

3. **Concentration:** Chris's extraordinary focus defines his exceptional photography. He doesn't just capture a shot; he captures *the* shot—the fleeting moment that tells a powerful story. Even in extreme conditions, his ability to zero in on the decisive moment transforms his work into compelling narratives, setting him apart.

4. **Composure:** Amid the chaos of blizzards in Iceland or the physical toll of cold water or high altitudes, Chris maintains his composure. By cultivating a deep well of inspiration and staying grounded through personal routines, he navigates stressful situations with resilience and calm.

5. **Commitment:** Chris's relentless hustle and willingness to sacrifice for his craft highlight his commitment. His dedication has been unwavering, from scraping pennies to fund his travels to continuously reinventing himself. He prioritizes projects that align with his values, ensuring his work remains meaningful and fulfilling.

YOUR CREATIVE TOOLKIT

Just as Chris Burkard exemplifies the 5 Cs of mental toughness in his journey as a photographer and artist, you too can develop these strengths. Here are practical tips and tools based on the 5 Cs of creativity, inspired by his journey.

1. **Courage:**
    - **Unmask Self-Sabotage:** Identify outdated voices from your past fueling self-sabotage. Those whispers of unworthiness are just echoes of old experiences. But here's the truth: you are worthy of success! Approach these thoughts with curiosity, not judgment. Ask yourself: "What part of me feels scared or vulnerable? What is it trying to convey, and how can I address it in a supportive way?"
    - **Dialogue with Doubts:** Don't let doubts hold you back—have a conversation. Journal about your doubts or speak them out loud in private. Remember, your worthiness of success is not up for debate. By giving voice to these fears, you can understand them better and see how they might hold you back.
    - **Build Distress Tolerance:** Develop your ability to tolerate distress and discomfort. Self-sabotage often stems from a fear of facing challenging or unfamiliar situations. But you are capable and deserving of growth! By gradually taking on more difficult and demanding tasks, you can build resilience and reduce the power of self-sabotage over time.
2. **Confidence:**
    - **Own Your Truths:** Craft a concise "I Know" list with seven to ten empowering statements that fuel your artistic conviction. Examples: "I know I create art that evokes emotion," "I know my unique perspective strengthens my work," "I know I can overcome any creative block," or "I know my artistic voice is valuable, even if it's different."

- **Prime for Success:** Before pivotal moments like auditions, project pitches, gallery openings, or live performances, review your "I Know" list to center yourself on core strengths, boosting confidence and mental readiness.
- **Carry Confidence:** Keep your "I Know" list handy—in your wallet, on your phone, or on your desk. Revisit these empowering statements whenever self-doubt creeps in to maintain creative momentum and confidence.

3. **Concentration:**
    - **Strengthen Your Focus: Visual Challenge:** These exercises will help you develop your ability to concentrate and stay focused. Visually challenge yourself intently for thirty seconds. Choose an object and observe it intensely, soaking up all the details, colors, and textures. It's like taking a mental snapshot.
    - **Strengthen Your Focus: Sound Adventure:** Embark on a sound adventure mindfully for thirty seconds. Close your eyes and immerse yourself in a world of sounds. Listen to the loudest noises and the softest whispers. Discover the layers of sound surrounding you.
    - **Strengthen Your Focus: Tactile Connection:** Connect with touch purposefully for thirty seconds. Feel the texture of an object, the softness of your clothes, or the solidity of the ground beneath your feet. Anchor your attention in the present moment.

4. **Composure:**
    - **Craft Your Creative Shield:** Close your eyes and envision a vibrant, protective barrier around your personal and creative space. Choose a color that inspires you, such as bold orange or calming blue.
    - **Activate Your Creative Defense:** When faced with negativity or pressure, visualize your shield radiating confidence and positivity. See it deflecting distractions and maintaining a clear, focused space for your creativity to flourish.

- **Strengthen Your Creative Resilience:** Make visualization a daily habit, even in times of calm. The more you practice, the stronger your mental shield becomes, empowering you to stay focused and creative under any circumstances.

5. **Commitment:**
   - **Ignite Your Morning Spark:** Energize your day with a creative gut check! Ask yourself: "How bad do you want it?" (HBDYWI). This daily question fans the flames of passion and clarifies your commitment to your art. Plus, it helps you tackle the not-so-glamorous tasks that come with the creative territory—think admin work, networking, or criticism.
   - **Constantly Remind Yourself:** Slap a sticky note or set your phone wallpaper with "HBDYWI." This constant reminder keeps your creative fire burning bright and your goals top of mind! It's also a helpful nudge when dealing with the less-than-ideal tasks you'd rather avoid—use it to push through the tedious stuff and stay focused on your artistic vision.
   - **Reignite with HBDYWI:** Hit a creative plateau? Revisit your "How bad do you want it?" question and let it rekindle your passion! Use it to push through temporary blocks, stay committed to your artistic vision, and remind yourself that even the less-glamorous tasks are worth it in the end.

CHARTING NEW CREATIVE FRONTIERS

*All that matters is that you are making something you
love, to the best of your ability, here and now.*
—Rick Rubin, producer

Forget scaling a single mountain peak—creativity is a vast, ever-changing landscape waiting to be explored. Throughout this book, you've been guided through the journeys of diverse trailblazers. From artists who conjure fantastical worlds to filmmakers who reshape genres, each story has offered a masterclass in nurturing creative talents and harnessing the power of your mindset.

YOUR CREATIVE ARSENAL

The inspiring stories in this book showcase the power of the 5 Cs: Courage, Confidence, Concentration, Composure, and Commitment. These are the cornerstones of peak creativity. These creative minds dared to take risks, capitalized on fleeting opportunities, maintained laser focus, stayed calm under pressure, and built a foundation of consistent practice. The pursuit of self-mastery through these principles involves continuously developing and refining these five key traits. By embracing the 5 Cs, you can elevate your creative potential and achieve a higher level of artistic excellence.

It's now your turn to take action! Each chapter concluded with a section titled "Your Creative Toolkit," packed with practical mental tips, tools, and techniques. This is your personal treasure trove of resources, designed to be revisited and applied time and again. As you refine your creative mind, this toolkit will be your constant companion.

Equipped with these powerful performance psychology principles and practical tools, you are now poised to unlock your full potential and gain a significant edge. Experiment with these techniques, make consistent practice your mantra, and watch them become the fuel that propels your creative journey. Embrace the challenge of self-mastery, guided by the 5 Cs.

FROM INSPIRATION TO IGNITION

Join the ranks of creative visionaries who have discovered the transformative power of "Create The Day" (CTD). This guiding principle fuels their relentless pursuit of artistic expression, empowering them to seize each day as an opportunity to leave an indelible mark on the world.

As you embark on your own creative journey, let the CTD mantra inspire you to transform every moment into a meaningful step on your artistic path, explore the vast landscape of creativity with courage and curiosity, and push the boundaries of your imagination.

Begin each day by reciting this uplifting artist's manifesto, celebrating creativity, self-expression, and personal growth. It's a potent reminder to stay true to yourself and embrace the artistic journey with mental toughness.

I spark my own fire,
Fueling every move I make.
Each touch, each word, each leap—
Refines and strengthens me.

Challenges sharpen my edge,
Successes ignite my confidence.
I create from the heart;
Each piece fuels my courage.

Driven by joy and passion,
I am the artist of my own life,
Crafting my destiny with each day.
Today, I own my vision,
Bringing it to life with purpose and intention.

As you speak these truths, feel the spark ignite within. It's a promise to yourself, a declaration of the art you will create. Live CTD fully:

- Schedule your creative time.
- Set goals.
- Take control.

Proactive planning prompts consistent progress, not last-minute scrambling. Make CTD your daily ritual, launching you on a lifelong creative adventure.

NAVIGATING YOUR CREATIVE VOYAGE

Consider this book your launchpad, not your finish line. Your creative mind is a vast, uncharted universe teeming with possibilities. Embrace the journey of exploration, where learning ignites curiosity, questioning triggers innovation, and venturing into the unknown leads to unexpected discoveries. The most captivating creative voyages are never truly over; they're lifelong expeditions of self-expression.

Unleash your inner artist. Let your creative fire ignite and illuminate your path. Weave your unique voice into the tapestry of the world, leaving an indelible mark—a testament to the relentless spirit that burns brightly within you.

Acknowledgments

DR. JIM AFREMOW

This book is the culmination of efforts, inspiration, and support from remarkable individuals whose contributions have been invaluable. I'm deeply grateful to my co-author, Phil White, whose brilliant interviewing skills and compelling storytelling have brought the rich narratives of this book to life. His collaboration has been essential to this project.

I also extend heartfelt thanks to the twelve talented creators who generously shared their stories, insights, and experiences with us, providing the foundation for this book.

I'm thankful for the guidance of our literary agent, Helen Zimmermann, whose dedication and expertise have been instrumental throughout the publication process. *The Creative's Mind* is our fifth successful collaboration together.

I appreciate the dedication and hard work of the team at BenBella Books, including:

- Victoria Carmody, our editor, for her insightful feedback and support
- Sarah Avinger, for her innovative design of the book's striking cover

- Jennifer Canzoneri, for her dynamic marketing strategies and publicity efforts
- Kim Broderick, our meticulous production editor
- Adrienne Lang, our publisher, for her leadership and commitment to excellence
- Alicia Kania, for expertly managing our content across platforms
- Madeline Grigg, for her invaluable assistance with endorsements

Additionally, a special thank-you to Elizabeth Smith for her exceptional line editing that greatly enhanced this project.

Each of you has played a pivotal role in this project, and I am immensely thankful.

On a personal note, I am profoundly grateful to my wife, Anne, and daughter, Maria Paz, for their unwavering love and support. Their patience and encouragement have been my anchor and inspiration throughout this journey.

PHIL WHITE

The waterman Laird Hamilton once said that alone he could have surfed some very good waves, but together with Dave Kalama and the rest of their crew he has been able to ride many of the greatest swells. I feel the same way about sharing the writing, researching, and interview experience with Jim Afremow for the second time. Some of my favorite memories among all my book experiences are of us geeking out about all the gold found in the interviews you've just read, and I'm grateful to call him co-author and friend. Jim's expertise as a psychologist and counselor were also crucial in creating all the practical takeaways.

This book would be nothing without the brilliant creators who kindly agreed to participate and share their powerful stories. I'll forever be grateful to Graham Thompson, BT, Keegan Hall, Tim Allen, Destin Daniel Cretton, Chris Burkard, Dom Streater, Stephen and Annette Wiltshire, David Greusel, Erik Larson, Ashley Stegon, and Suzannah Bianco. I hope you enjoy taking a peek inside their minds and creative processes as much as Jim and I did, and that their words of wisdom stick with you.

Several people were instrumental behind the scenes in setting up these interviews. I'm grateful to Dean Nelson for putting us in touch with Destin Daniel Cretton and Amy Tajiri for scheduling a Zoom call with him. We're also indebted to Lacy Transeau for finding time with BT, Penny Gerald for reconnecting us with Erik Larson, and Mike Sandifer for setting up a call with Chris Burkard.

The old adage is that it takes a village to raise a child, and that's also true for bringing a book to life. I'm thankful for the care, diligence, and expertise of the BenBella team, including Victoria Carmody, Elizabeth Smith, Leah Wilson, Glenn Yeffeth, Sarah Avinger, Jennifer Canzoneri, Kim Broderick, Adrienne Lang, Alicia Kania, and Madeline Grigg.

I'm also blessed to have creative people in my daily life who have kept me going on this twenty-year writing journey. My lovely wife, Nicole, doesn't merely have my heart but is also an endlessly inventive fashion designer and the unsung hero of the editing process. It was also her idea to interview Destin and Dom. My sons, Johnny and Harry, are animators and filmmakers and I hope this book prompts other young people to become the artists and storytellers of tomorrow.

Other family members have been supportive and encouraging along the way, including Jacqui, Barrie, Debbie, Meg, my father, Cherie, Ollie, Lisa, Mike, Mollie, Nick, Janice, Randy, David, Nicole, and Hilde. I'm also lucky to have some fantastic friends in my corner, including Brett Chalmers, Ben Spicer, Rodger Fernandez, Cory Maxwell, Dan Vanderpool, Henry Worcester, Tom Seibold, Justen Wack, Kevin Kerr, Ryan Parrott, Rorke Denver, Kevin Kerr, Craig Babcock, Jon Manley, Brett Yoho, Matt Cormier, and James Geering. Finally. I'd like to thank God for the gift of this project and putting all these wonderful people in my life.

Unlocking Creativity

The Science Behind Mindfulness and Mental Training

Exploring the science behind mindfulness and mental training reveals how these practices can enhance your creativity, from mindfulness exercises and mental imagery techniques to strategies for overcoming obstacles like imposter syndrome. Numerous studies support the importance of mindset and mental training; the following examples are just a glimpse into the world of research on creativity. Further exploration of these practices can be a valuable tool for anyone seeking to unlock their creative potential.

SHARPENING YOUR CREATIVE EDGE WITH MINDFULNESS

Recent research highlights a strong connection between mindfulness and creativity. A 2014 study found that a short program of integrative body-mind training (IBMT), blending mindfulness and relaxation techniques, significantly improved creative output and emotional control. Just 30 minutes a day for one week boosted participants' divergent thinking, a key element of creativity, while enhancing their emotional management skills.[1] This finding supports the mindfulness and relaxation practices outlined in *The Creative's Mind*, suggesting that incorporating mindfulness and relaxation into your daily routine can be a game-changer for sparking creativity.

A 2012 study from Leiden University revealed the power of a specific type of mindfulness known as "open-monitoring meditation."[2] Unlike focused meditation, this technique involves observing your thoughts and sensations without judgment. The result? Participants who practiced this technique were better at generating a wider range of ideas and making unique connections between them. This finding resonates with the concept of brainstorming, where fostering a nonjudgmental space for exploration is key to generating new ideas.

ENHANCING CREATIVE PERFORMANCE THROUGH MENTAL SKILLS TRAINING

A 2014 study published in *Psychology of Well-Being* emphasized the importance of mental preparation in creative endeavors. The study demonstrated that a brief mental skills training program significantly enhanced the performance and resilience of music students at the Melbourne Conservatorium of Music.[3]

Specifically, the findings showed reduced performance anxiety, better preparation, and increased courage. Notably, the "centering" technique helped students manage their physiological responses and focus on key performance cues. This research underscores the value of mental skills training in creative pursuits, highlighting how a calm and focused mindset is paramount in achieving excellence.

CONQUERING IMPOSTER SYNDROME

Imposter syndrome, the feeling of being a fraud despite your achievements, is a common hurdle for many creatives. Research from the

International Journal of Behavioral Science found that approximately 70 percent of people experience imposter syndrome at some point.[4] This can lead to chronic self-doubt and can hinder creative performance. The good news is that addressing these feelings through cognitive restructuring and self-compassion practices can help mitigate their negative impact. *The Creative's Mind* delves into imposter syndrome and provides strategies to combat it, aligning with the research on self-compassion.

BUILDING SELF-BELIEF WITH SELF-AFFIRMATION

Another fascinating 2013 study, from the University of Texas, highlighted the role of self-affirmation in combating imposter syndrome and enhancing mental resilience.[5] Participants who engaged in self-affirmation exercises, where they wrote about their core values and important personal attributes, showed reduced stress levels and improved performance in creative tasks. This suggests that regular self-affirmation can be a powerful tool for maintaining creativity and confidence in the face of self-doubt. Techniques for positive self-talk and affirmations are explored in *The Creative's Mind*, supported by this research on self-affirmation.

CULTIVATING YOUR CREATIVE MINDSET NOW AND IN THE FUTURE

By incorporating mindfulness practices, mental training techniques, and strategies to address psychological challenges, you can cultivate a mental state that is more conducive to creative thinking. Explore the tools and exercises throughout this book, which are firmly supported by the research findings. In addition, further applied interventions and research on sport and performance psychology can be found in *The Champion's Mind: How Great Athletes Think, Train, and Thrive* (2014), by Jim Afremow; *The Champion's Comeback: How Great Athletes Recover, Reflect, and Reignite* (2016), by Jim Afremow; *The Young Champion's Mind: How to Think,*

Train, and Thrive Like an Elite Athlete (2018), by Jim Afremow; and *The Leader's Mind: How Great Leaders Prepare, Perform, and Prevail* (2021), by Jim Afremow with Phil White.

SOURCES

1. Xiaoqian Ding, Yi-Yuan Tang, Rongxiang Tang, and Michael I. Posner, "Improving Creativity Performance by Short-Term Meditation," *Behavioral and Brain Functions* 10, no. 1 (2014): 1–8.
2. Lorenza S. Colzato, Ayca Ozturk, and Bernhard Hommel, "Meditate to Create: The Impact of Focused-Attention and Open-Monitoring Training on Convergent and Divergent Thinking," *Frontiers in Psychology* 3 (2012): 116.
3. M. S. Osborne, D. J. Greene, and D. T. Immel, "Managing Performance Anxiety and Improving Mental Skills in Conservatoire Students through Performance Psychology Training: A Pilot Study," *Psychology of Well-Being* 4, no. 18 (2014).
4. Jaruwan Sakulku, "The Impostor Phenomenon," *International Journal of Behavioral Science* 6, no. 1 (2011): 75–97.
5. J. David Creswell et al., "Self-Affirmation Improves Problem-Solving under Stress," *PLoS One* 8, no. 5 (2013): e62593.

Appendix 2

The 5 Cs of Creativity

Words from the Masters

The creative path requires a unique blend of skills and mindsets. Here, famous creatives share their insights on the 5 Cs that fuel artistic endeavors:

Courage

1. "Without courage, you can't write the truth."
   —Margaret Atwood, novelist
2. "It takes courage to grow up and become who you really are."
   —E. E. Cummings, poet
3. "Courage starts with showing up and letting ourselves be seen."
   —Brené Brown, researcher and author
4. "Life shrinks or expands in proportion to one's courage."
   —Anaïs Nin, writer
5. "Only those who will risk going too far can possibly find out how far one can go." —T. S. Eliot, poet
6. "You can't be that kid standing at the top of the waterslide,

overthinking it. You have to go down the chute." —Tina Fey, comedian

7. "Fear is like a bully—the more you confront it, the smaller it gets." —Halsey, singer

8. "You don't want to be the best at what you do, you want to be the only one." —Jerry Garcia, musician

9. "I'd be more frightened by not using whatever abilities I'd been given. I'd be more frightened by procrastination and laziness." —Denzel Washington, actor

10. "The soul should always stand ajar, ready to welcome the ecstatic experience." —Emily Dickinson, poet

Confidence

1. "Your self-worth is determined by you. You don't have to depend on someone telling you who you are." —Beyoncé, singer

2. "Confidence is a quiet inner knowledge—not arrogant showmanship." —Iris Apfel, fashion icon

3. "Doubt is a killer. You have to know what you stand for and go for it." —Chris Rock, comedian

4. "I always knew I was a star, and now the rest of the world seems to agree with me." —Freddie Mercury, musician

5. "Our doubts are traitors, and make us lose the good we oft might win, by fearing to attempt." —William Shakespeare, playwright

6. "Confidence is key. Sometimes, you need to look like you're confident even when you're not." —Emma Stone, actress

7. "Don't let them take your power. Don't let them take your confidence." —Usher, singer

8. "I am who I am, and that's all I need to be." —Kendrick Lamar, rapper

9. "You are your best thing." —Toni Morrison, novelist

10. "I celebrate myself, and sing myself." —Walt Whitman, poet

Concentration

1. "Concentration is the secret of strength." —Ralph Waldo Emerson, essayist
2. "Where the attention goes, the energy flows." —James Redfield, author
3. "To pay attention, this is our endless and proper work." —Mary Oliver, poet
4. "Whenever you want to achieve something, keep your eyes open, concentrate, and know exactly what you want. No one can hit their target with their eyes closed." —Paulo Coelho, author
5. "Trifles make perfection, and perfection is no trifle." —Michelangelo, sculptor
6. "I find that the harder I work on something, the more I can see its shape. "—Georgia O'Keeffe, painter
7. "I get into a zone and forget everything else. It's like being in a trance." —Yo-Yo Ma, musician
8. "Forever is composed of Nows." —Emily Dickinson, poet
9. "The quieter you become, the more you can hear." —Rumi, poet and Sufi mystic
10. "The world is full of magic things patiently waiting for our senses to grow sharper." —W. B. Yeats, poet

Composure

1. "The mind is its own place, and in itself can make a heaven of hell, a hell of heaven." —John Milton, poet
2. "Calmness is the cradle of power." —Josiah Gilbert Holland, poet
3. "Grace is finding a way to be comfortable in your own skin, recognizing that you have worth." —Misty Copeland, ballet dancer
4. "The true secret of happiness lies in taking a genuine interest in all the details of daily life." —William Morris, designer
5. "You may encounter many defeats, but you must not be

defeated. In fact, you must use each defeat as a stepping-stone to a higher place." —Maya Angelou, poet

6. "Be like water, my friend." —Bruce Lee, martial artist
7. "The best way to stay calm and composed is to remain present in the moment." —Samuel L. Jackson, actor
8. "In three words I can sum up everything I've learned about life: it goes on." —Robert Frost, poet
9. "The best way to cheer yourself up is to try to cheer somebody else up." —Mark Twain, author
10. "I am not afraid of storms, for I am learning how to sail my ship." —Louisa May Alcott, author

Commitment

1. "Commitment is an act, not a word." —Jean-Paul Sartre, philosopher
2. "It takes twenty years to make an overnight success." —Ed Sheeran, musician
3. "I never dreamed about success. I worked for it." —Estée Lauder, entrepreneur
4. "The most important thing about art is to work. Nothing else matters except sitting down every day and trying." —Steven Pressfield, author
5. "Success isn't about the end result, it's about what you learn along the way." —Vera Wang, fashion designer
6. "A goal is a dream with a finish line." —Duke Ellington, musician
7. "Without commitment, you cannot have depth in anything." —Neil Strauss, author
8. "Ever tried. Ever failed. No matter. Try again. Fail again. Fail better." —Samuel Beckett, playwright
9. "I always wanted to be someone better the next day than I was the day before." —Sidney Poitier, actor
10. "Perseverance is failing nineteen times and succeeding the twentieth." —Julie Andrews, actress

About the Authors

Dr. Jim Afremow is a leading high-performance consultant and the best-selling author of *The Champion's Mind*, *The Champion's Comeback*, *The Young Champion's Mind*, and *The Leader's Mind* (co-authored with Phil White). With over two decades of experience, he provides mental skills training and leadership services to elite athletes, teams, coaches, and corporate professionals across a wide range of sports and fields.

Dr. Afremow has worked with top-tier athletes from the NFL, MLB, NBA, NHL, UFC, MLS, PGA Tour, LPGA Tour, and WNBA, as well as U.S. and international Olympians. His experience includes roles as a staff sport psychologist for the Greek softball and Indian field hockey Olympic teams, and as the peak performance coordinator and mental skills coach for the San Francisco Giants.

He co-hosts the *Champion Conversations Podcast* with Phil White. Dr. Afremow lives in Eugene, Oregon, with his wife, Anne, and their daughter, Maria Paz. For more information, visit drjimafremow.com.

Phil White is an Emmy-nominated writer and the author of *The Leader's Mind* with Jim Afremow, *Unplugged* with Andy Galpin and Brian Mackenzie, *Waterman 2.0* with Kelly Starrett, *Game Changer* with Fergus Connolly, and *The 17 Hour Fast* with Frank Merritt. He also tells stories for elite companies like KALA, TrainingPeaks, Momentous, Ergodriven, Vitality Blueprint, Teamworks, XPT, StrongFirst, TRX, and Onnit. Phil lives with his wife and two sons in Evergreen, Colorado. Start a conversation with him @PhilWhiteBooks and philwhitebooks.com.